Clematis
THE MONTANAS

Clematis

THE MONTANAS

A book for Gardeners

John Howells

Photographs by the Author
Consultant – Wim Snoeijer

ISBN 1 870673 51 4

British Library Cataloguing–in–Publication Data
A catalogue record for this book is available from
the British Library

Published by Garden Art Press,
a division of Antique Collectors' Club Ltd

Frontispiece: 'Perle d'Azur' on 'Mayleen' foliage.

Printed in China
by Antique Collectors' Club Ltd., Sandy Lane, Old Martlesham,
Woodbridge, Suffolk IP12 4SD, UK

THE ANTIQUE COLLECTORS' CLUB

Formed in 1966, the Antique Collectors' Club is now a world-renowned publisher of top quality books for the collector. It also publishes the only independently-run monthly antiques magazine, *Antique Collecting*, which rose quickly from humble beginnings to a network of worldwide subscribers.

The magazine, whose motto is *For Collectors-By Collectors-About Collecting*, is aimed at collectors interested in widening their knowledge of antiques both by increasing their awareness of quality and by discussion of the factors influencing prices.

Subscription to *Antique Collecting* is open to anyone interested in antiques and subscribers receive ten issues a year. Well-illustrated articles deal with practical aspects of collecting and provide numerous tips on prices, features of value, investment potential, fakes and forgeries. Offers of related books at special reduced prices are also available only to subscribers.

In response to the enormous demand for information on 'what to pay', ACC introduced in 1968 the famous price guide series. The first title, *The Price Guide to Antique Furniture* (since renamed *British Antique Furniture: Price Guide and Reasons for Values*), is still in constant demand. Since those pioneering days, ACC has gone from strength to strength, publishing many of today's standard works of reference on all things antique and collectable, from *Tiaras* to *20th Century Ceramic Designers in Britain*.

Not only has ACC continued to cater strongly for its original audience, it has also branched out to produce excellent titles on many subjects including art reference, architecture, garden design, gardens, and textiles. All ACC's publications are available through bookshops worldwide and a catalogue is available free of charge from the addresses below.

For further information please contact:

ANTIQUE COLLECTORS' CLUB

www.antique-acc.com

Sandy Lane, Old Martlesham
Woodbridge, Suffolk IP12 4SD, UK
Tel: 01394 389950 Fax: 01394 389999
Email: info@antique-acc.com
or
Antique Collectors' Club Ltd
Eastworks, 116 Pleasant Street - Suite #60B
Easthampton, MA 01027
Tel: (413) 529 0861 Fax: (413) 529 0862
Email: info@antiquecc.com

ACKNOWLEDGEMENTS

It is a pleasure to record and thank a number of willing helpers in the writing of this book.

Professor Simon Owen of the Royal Botanic Gardens, Kew, made it possible for me to visit the Wallich Collection in the Herbarium and supplied a reproduction of *Clematis punduana*. The Curator of the Herbarium at the Natural History Museum gave access to their collection and supplied photocopies of the Museum's *Clematis montana* specimens. The Herbarium of the Linnean Society, now being reorganised, supplied excellent illustrations of *Clematis montana*. Wim Snoeijer made the translation of the original description of *Clematis spoonerii*. Denis Bradshaw, Curator of the first National Montana Collection made access possible to the Collection and was free with his unique knowledge of the montanas. Steve Gilsenan, Curator of the current National Collection of Montanas also supplied information. My thanks to Beng Sundström of Magnus Johnson's Plantskola AB for permission to publish a map of the world distribution of *Clematis montana*.

The great majority of the photographs are by the author and they were supplemented by Wim Snoeijer's photograph of *Clematis tongluensis*, Brewster Rogerson's photograph of 'Brewster', Robin Mitchell's photographs of his unique new montanas, and the late Jack Elliot's photograph of *Clematis chrysocoma* (dwarf). I would not have been able to study Montana 'Veitch' in my garden except for the generous gift of a plant from Mr John Philips taken as a cutting from what is probably the only plant of 'Veitch' then known to exist. To the intrepid Sue and Bleddyn Wynne-Jones of Crug Farm Plants I am indebted for information on *Clematis montana yuishan*. The doyen of Japanese clematarians, Mr Y. Aihara, gave me valuable advice with photographs of the montanas in Japan. To the Curator of the Logan Botanic Garden, Scotland, I am indebted for information on *Clematis montana* 'Bi-color'. Sheila Chapman introduced me to the merits of two of her introductions — *Clematis montana* 'Unity' and *Clematis montana* 'Christine'. It was a surprising experience to visit the garden of Mr Lawrence Banks at Hergest Croft Garden and see a massive plant of *Clematis* 'Wilsonii' in flower.

I have gained much profit from the authoritative support and advice of my Consultant, Wim Snoeijer, lately of Leiden University, and of Van Zoest Clematis. Even with his expert help errors may have crept into the book; for these the author is entirely responsible. It has been a pleasure to collaborate with Diana Steel and her team at Garden Art Press. Constant enthusiastic support came as always from my literary assistant, Mrs Janet Hodge, the epitome of efficiency and literary expertise.

CONTENTS

Acknowledgements   6

Introduction   8

Chapter   I   Characteristics of the Montana Group   10

Chapter   II   The Finding of *Clematis montana*   28

Chapter   III   The Montanas described   45

Chapter   IV   Supplementary List of Montanas   124

Chapter   V   Cultivation of the Montanas   142

Chapter   VI   Displaying Your Montanas   173

Chapter   VII   Historical Notes   200

Index   209

INTRODUCTION

Winter brings a sombre note to the garden and we look to the spring to lighten up the vista. The plant, beyond all plants, that achieves this is the montana clematis. In a flash there is drama. Huge sweeps of colour involving thousands of small flowers climb into trees, cover walls and embellish shrubs bringing you out of the house to witness the spectacle. Although no one montana clematis flowers for long, (but longer than, say, wisteria), a carefully selected sequence of montanas, however, can provide flowers and colour from April through to September. At first colour catches the eye and, as you approach, many of the montanas also produce an overwhelming fragrance. Montanas are known for their massive size – usually a great virtue – but for smaller gardens we now have smaller plants which are still able to make an impact within a restricted space.

Colour may attract the gardener to a plant but growing it reveals other virtues. This group of clematis are vigorous, easy to plant, easy to grow. They are free of stem rot (clematis wilt). Pruning is easy. When not in flower the gardener can use the large area of greenery of the plant in his garden scheme – as a background to other plants or to camouflage what might otherwise be an eyesore. In the autumn, as a bonus, some montanas produce attractive seed heads. No wonder the montanas are the most popular group in all clematis, the most eminent Queen of Climbers. One can reflect also that a montana can be a friend for a lifetime. Such is their longevity.

This book is for gardeners who need to know more about the general features of this group of clematis. They need to know, for example, which montanas are available on the market, their strong and weak points and which are best suited for their pariticular purpose. They need to know how to cultivate this group of plants and how best to display them. Every plant has a history and it is a particularly fascinating one in the case of montanas. Everything the gardener needs to know is provided here.

The author has studied the montana plants in his garden over many years. Each was purchased from reputable nurserymen in Europe. The surest way of evaluating garden worthiness of a plant is to grow it for some years in the garden. The author has no commercial interest in the montanas. Thus he gives a detached evaluation.

Clematis montana was brought to Europe by Francis Buchanan in 1805. That event is celebrated by this book which is published to mark its bicentenary. Buchanan's discovery has brought delight and joy to many gardeners throughout the world. The book contains the first account of this notable finding.

CHAPTER I

CHARACTERISTICS OF THE MONTANA GROUP

The Genus *Clematis*

It may be useful to have a general idea of the features of the genus *Clematis* to which the montana group belongs (Figure I).

Most of the clematis are climbing members of the Ranunculaceae family which includes such flowers as the aconites, hellebores, anemones, buttercups, columbines, larkspurs and delphiniums.

The genus *Clematis*, as we shall see later, can be divided for the gardener into twelve groups, of which the montanas are one. Of its twelve groups one is herbaceous, the rest, including the montanas and with a few exceptions, climb. Eleven groups, including the montanas, are usually deciduous while the first group to flower in the flowering year is evergreen.

The clematis flower has one striking and unusual feature: it has no sepals which instead take on the function of the petals and are termed 'tepals'. Otherwise it conforms to a normal flower structure and in addition to the tepals, has male parts (stamens), and female parts (pistils). Clematis are classed as woody plants since the green soft stems usually soon become woody, adding to their hardiness. Clematis leaves usually grow opposite each other on stems; in the Montana groups there are usually three leaflets (ternate); in the other groups they can take on many forms and may be much divided or even simple.

The clematis has a long history. When European herbals came to be written from the sixteenth century onwards the clematis was always mentioned and described although its medicinal value was small. Clematis became popular as gardeners turned to leisure gardening and the beauty of the clematis was recognised.

Most countries in the temperate regions of the Northern and Southern hemispheres have native clematis. *The International Clematis Register and Checklist 2002* contains the names of about 2,750 clematis.

With cross-breeding of clematis belonging to the same group, and to a lesser extent, between groups, new clematis appeared over time. Clematis enjoyed an enormous boost in its fortunes in the mid-nineteenth century when, as a consequence of the increased interest in plant hunting, the native species, especially the viticellas, were crossed with recently discovered large flowered clematis from China and Japan. The most successful cross was with *Clematis lanuginosa* from China. So large and lovely were the new large clematis that there was an enormous increase in production. Unfortunately, as we know today, *C. lanuginosa* and other clematis used in hybridising, was

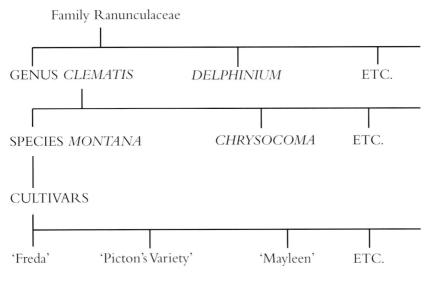

Figure I.   **Table of the Family Ranunculaceae**

susceptible to stem rot (clematis wilt), and that weakness passed to the Early Group of Large Flowered clematis. This group still suffers from that weakness today. The montanas, however, are free from stem rot.

Grouping Clematis for Garden Purposes

The gardener needs to know the general characteristics of the various groups of clematis so that he can take their special qualities into account when he plans his garden. The gardener also needs to know where the montanas fit in the world of clematis.

At one time clematis were grouped or classified according to their pruning requirements. Though useful information for pruning, it told us nothing about the general characteristics of the clematis. Here I use a new, more convenient and easily understood classification (see Table 1). Clematis are divided into twelve groups. The twelve are described here in the approximate sequence of flowering. The first starts blooming in early winter. The twelfth ends its blooming in late autumn. Knowing the twelve groups is the key to the understanding of clematis. A brief summary of each group follows in Table 1 (overleaf).

1.   Howells, J. 'A Gardener's Classification of Clematis'. 1992. *The Clematis*, p.14. Refined in *Choosing Your Clematis*, 2000. Antique Collectors' Club.

TABLE 1   THE TWELVE CLEMATIS GROUPS

These groups are in the approximate order of flowering.

1. The Evergreen group – the tender group – e.g. 'Apple Blossom'
2. The Alpina group – the group of single bells – e.g. 'Jacqueline du Pré'
3. The Macropetala group – the group of double bells – e.g. 'Markham's Pink'
4. The Montana Group – the group of giant clematis – e.g. 'Mayleen'
5. The Rockery group – the group of dwarf clematis – e.g. 'Joe'
6. The Early Large-Flowered group – the 'dinner plate' group – e.g. 'Nelly Moser'
7. The Late Large-Flowered group – the 'tea plate' group – e.g. 'Jackmanii'
8. The Herbaceous group – the border group – e.g. 'Durandii'
9. The Viticella group – the easy group - e.g. 'Madame Julia Correvon'
10. The Texensis group – the group of climbing tulips – e.g. 'Princess Diana'
11. The Orientalis group – the yellow group – e.g. 'Bill MacKenzie'
12. The Late mixed group – the autumn group – e.g. 'Triternata Rubromarginata'

The Name

'Montana' stands for 'of the mountain'. The name *C. montana* was first used by Francis Buchanan, who discovered the plant, and details were first published by De Candolle in his *Systema*, Volume I, in 1817. The original name stands, ever since. David Don, in his *Prodromus Florae Nepalensis*, 1825, however, listed it as *C. anemoniflora*. The original *C. montana* has given its name to a cultivated group of plants of similar habit – the Montana Group or, in popular English, the montanas.

Natural Habitat

The mountains of India, Burma, China and Taiwan. (See Figure II)

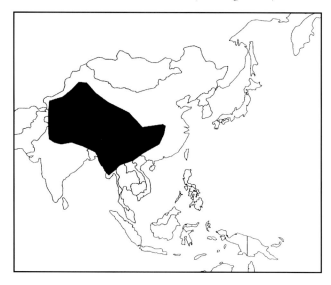

Figure II.
Diagram -
Distribution map for
subsection Montanae
(from Magnus
Johnson, *The Genus
Clematis,* p.369).

Historical

Amongst the lore of the literature on clematis is the statement that '*Clematis montana* was introduced to Europe by Lady Amherst in 1831'. This myth persists to this day in the literature. The author's research reveals that *Clematis montana* was discovered by Dr Francis Buchanan at Chitlong, Nepal, on 11 April 1802 and introduced to Europe in 1805. For more information see Chapter II 'The Finding of Clematis montana'.

C. montana grandiflora soon joined the group after it had been discovered by N. Wallich, or one of his collectors, before 1844. *Clematis chrysochoma* joined the group in 1884 after it was discovered by Abbé Delavay in China. Further very meritorious entrants were *C. montana rubens* and *C. montana* var. *wilsonii* found and introduced by E. H. Wilson in 1900. *C.* x *vedrariensis* joined from a cross made by Vilmorin at Verrières, near Paris, before 1914. Since then many hybrids joined the group and their origin will be found with the description of each plant.

Gardener's Classification of the Montanas

A convenient grouping is to think of three sub-groups. (1) The large main Montana sub-group; (2) the small Chrysocoma sub-group of two plants; (3) the small Vedrariensis sub-group of four plants. The features of the two latter sub-groups in general resemble that of the first larger main sub-group.

The large Montana sub-group can be further sub-divided in terms of vigour, time of flowering, fragrance, height achieved, foliage, etc. But the most valuable entity for identification for gardeners is that in terms of colouring – white, pale pink, pink, deep pink. That will be followed here. (See Chapter III.)

Habit

Members of the montana group are deciduous climbers, with the flowers appearing from the old wood. The plants can be very vigorous and the strongest are able to climb to 9m. (30ft.) and beyond. Fortunately, some montanas will only reach 2.4–3m. (8–10ft.) and these are very suitable for small gardens. The spread of the plant depends on the way in which it is grown by the gardener. If stems are encouraged to grow horizontally rather than vertically, the spread can be as great as the height of the plant.

PLATE 1.
'Odorata' fades as it matures.

Flowers

The flower is usually single and spreading. A few are semi-double or double. The flower appears on long stalks.

Like all clematis, the flowers of the Montanas have no sepals, these having taken over the function of petals. These are called 'tepals' and are four in number. Exceptions are the double-flowered montanas, which in addition to tepals have tepal-like pistillodes.

The stamens are usually yellow. With the exception of 'Jacqui', the double flowers do not have stamens.

The colour of the tepals varies from white to pale pink to pink to deep pink.

As the flower matures the colour of the tepals can fade. (Plate 1) Prolonged dull weather at the time of flowering can lead to flowers being paler than usual.

As for scent there appears to be no agreed way of defining fragrance. To say 'pleasant' tells you nothing. Scents, therefore, are compared to another flower such as lavender, or a plant like mint, a tree like hawthorn, to a fruit like lemon, to an animal scent like musk, or seeds such as ginger, or to a familiar product like chocolate. Sometimes the best we can do is to indicate strength such as weak, strong or very strong.

The flowers may be followed by attractive seed heads.(Plate 2)

The plant is monoecious, having male and female parts in the same flower. The stamens, male parts of the flower, are usually well developed. In the female part of the flower, the pistil, there are a number of carpels where seeds are produced. Typically, the flowers are 4–6 cm. (1½–2⅜in.) across.

The flowers usually appear singly or, more commonly, as a cluster, from between leaf stalks.(Plate 3)

PLATE 2.
Seeds of 'Rubens'.

PLATE 3.
Cluster of buds in 'Rosea'.

Foliage

PLATE 4.
The ternate leaf of a montana.

The leaves are ternate, i.e. they make three leaflets.(Plate 4) The edge of the leaflets are usually broken but they can occasionally be entire. There are no bracts. The colour range of the leaf is from light green to deep bronze. Young leaves in particular tend to be bronze. In general, the lighter the leaf the lighter the flower colour; the deeper the leaf colour the deeper the flower colour. There are a few that break this rule, e.g. 'Elten', 'New Dawn'and 'East Malling'.

Roots

In clematis most groups have fibrous roots (Plate 5), while a few have lace-like roots. The montanas have fibrous roots and these need to be treated with care.

PLATE 5.
Fibrous roots.

Flowering Time

Most montanas start flowering in the spring. However, some flower in late spring and one even in early autumn.

There is a sequence of flowering. *C. gracilifolia* opens the season. Then comes the main montana sub-group. They are followed by the Vedrariensis sub-group and the Chrysocoma sub-group is last. In the main montana sub-group 'Alexander', 'Elizabeth', 'Freda', 'Odorata' and 'Warwickshire Rose' come first. Then comes the majority. One to two weeks after their flowering, 'White Fragrance' and the doubles come into flower.

In late summer comes *C. wilsonii*. 'Continuity' produces a second blooming in early autumn. Thus a montana can be in bloom somewhere in the garden over a period of five months.

The flowering period for a particular montana tends to be short – two to four weeks. Longest flowering are 'Marjorie', 'Olga', *C. chrysocoma* and 'Continuity'. Careful choosing of a sequence of plant flowerings can provide colour for a number of months, e.g. the following in order – *C. gracilifolia* 'Freda', 'Mayleen', 'Broughton Star', *C. chrysocoma*, 'White Fragrance', 'Continuity' and *C. wilsonii*.

Hardiness

There are certain essentials that a gardener needs to know about his garden, for example soil type, and the direction of the prevailing wind. Another essential piece of information is the hardiness zone in which the garden lies. Montanas need an average annual minimum temperature above -18°C (0°F). In the USA this is Zone 7–9. See a discussion of hardiness zones later in Chapter V.

The montanas, with the evergreen and rockery groups, are the most tender of clematis. In general the main montana sub-group is more hardy than the chrysocoma and vedrariensis sub-groups. However, susceptible plants can be protected by growing them in sheltered positions, away from cold prevailing winds, e.g. a belt of evergreen trees between the prevailing wind and the plants can help survival. Protection will be discussed in Chapter V.

While montanas can perish in sub-zero temperatures, the most common damage to a montana, in the areas in which they grow, are late frosts. These will not kill the plant or even damage the foliage but they can destroy the buds and hence deprive the plant of flowering that year. This happened in the U.K. in the spring of 1982 and again in 1990 and 1997.

Pruning

This is minimal. Gardeners should allocate a space for each of their montanas so that they do not intrude on other plants. When the montana spreads out of its space it can then be pruned back, after flowering, to the space allotted it. If a montana has been properly grown with a number of trunks then in old plants one trunk can be removed periodically to encourage new growth. (See Chapter V 'Cultivation of the Montanas'.)

Uses

The plants should be given enough room to produce the drama that they are capable of. They can be used to cover physical structures such as walls, pillars, fences, roofs. They are particularly effective growing into large trees (even evergreens).(See Chapter VI 'Displaying your Montanas'.)

Disease resistance

There is no disease or pest particular to the montanas. They are free of stem rot (clematis wilt).

Soil requirements

They will flourish in most soils although there must be an abundant water supply. Making such huge plants they also flourish with ample manuring. (See Chapter V 'Cultivation of the Montanas'.)

Points That Favour the Montanas

The immense vigour of the plants.
The wonderful mass of colour they produce.
Many are scented.
A sequence of flowering montanas will provide colour for a long time.
Montanas are free of stem rot (clematis wilt).

Points Against the Montanas

These are minimal:
An individual montana has a short period of flowering. Therefore it is advisable to grow a number for successive periods of flowering.
In some areas they are liable to frost damage.
They have no leaves in winter therefore plant in places not visible from your windows. (See Chapter VI 'Displaying your Montanas'.)

AGM

This stands for Award of Garden Merit (AGM) of the Royal Horticultural Society, UK. Such plants should have the following qualities:
•   outstanding excellence for garden decoration or use
•   available in the trade
•   of good constitution
•   requiring neither highly specialist growing conditions nor care.
Not to have achieved this accolade, however, does not imply that a plant is not meritorious. Many have not been put forward for trial. The AGM has been awarded to 'Broughton Star', 'Elizabeth', 'Freda', 'Grandiflora', 'Mayleen', 'Rubens' and 'Tetrarose'.

Nomenclature

Clematis nurseries take infinite care to be sure that their plants are true to name. But, inevitably, in a complex field of inter-breeding over two centuries, areas of uncertainty can appear. Difficulties arise from a number of sources. The montanas are often grown from seed, as they grow readily in this way. There may be differences in the seedlings from the parent plant but they may be given the name of the parent plant. The converse may happen. Differences from the parent plant may be very small but the seedling is given a new name. Plants may be lost but when found again are mis-identified, e.g. *C. chrysocoma* var. *spooneri* was not that plant but *C*. 'Grandiflora'.

After careful study some changes are suggested here. The *Clematis wilsonii* flowering with the main group of montanas bears no resemblance to any plant discovered by Wilson. However, it is most splendid and has been given the new name of 'White Fragrance', descriptive of its habit.

The true *Clematis* var. *wilsonii* flowers two months later in the year. This plant, however, is the same as 'Peveril'.

Clematis 'Superba' has a white flower and was introduced by Jackman's in 1915. The word 'Superba' is used today for a pink plant; this may have been a plant given this name in The Netherlands some years ago after a trial of montanas, but the name was withdrawn in The Netherlands and replaced with 'New Dawn'. The true white 'Superba' was re-introduced from Sweden and is now grown in both the Netherlands and U.K.

C. montana E.M.F. is so distinctive, and so different from 'Rubens', as to merit standing on its own as 'East Malling'.

Here the term 'Montana Group' is used to cover the main Montana sub-group plus two related sub-groups – the Chrysocoma sub-group and the Vedrariensis sub-group.

Botanical Classification of the Montanas

By Christopher Grey-Wilson there is a sub-section Montanae under the sub-genus Cheiropsis.
By Magnus Johnson there is a sub-section Montanae under Section Cheiropsis.
By Wim Snoeijer there is a sub-section Montanae under Section Cheiropsis of sub-genus Clematis.

Recommended Selections of Montanas

As not everyone has the same taste in flowers, there is scope for varying choices. The lists below will not disappoint.

One only: 'Mayleen'

For LARGE gardens:

C. chrycoscoma	'Mayleen'
'Elizabeth'	C. montana
'Grandiflora'	'White Fragrance'

For SMALL gardens:

'Broughton Star'	'Picton's Variety'
'Freda'	'Rubens'
'Jacqui'	'Tetrarose'

For the Connoisseur with a sympathetic climate:

'Continuity'	'Veitch'
C. gracilifolia	C. wilsonii
'Rosea'	

Scent – very scented:

'Elizabeth'	'Pink Perfection'
'Fragrant Spring'	'Rubens'
'Mayleen'	'Vera'
'Odorata'	'White Fragrance'

A National Collection of Clematis Montana

In the U.K. a new national collection is being established at Meols Hall, Botanic Road, Churchtown, Southport, PR9 7LZ. Meols Hall is also the home of the prestigious Southport Spring Show. Already planted is a covered walkway displaying *C. montana wilsonii*. In 2003 fifty additional plantings of montanas had been made and this will continue in the future. It is expected that the collection will be recognised by the National Council for the Conservation of Plants and Gardens (NCCPG), a body that co-ordinates and sponsors conservation in the U.K.

The Curator is Steve Gilsenan, ex-committee member of The British Clematis Society and proprietor of County Clematis Nursery, Burscough, Ormskirk, West Lancashire, U.K. Viewing of the collection is by arrangement with the Curator at Tel/Fax: 0151–5203310.

The collection supersedes the fine national collection of montanas held at Busheyfields Nursery, Herne Bay, Kent, U.K. There, for many years, the Curator was Denis Bradshaw, an ex-Chairman of The British Clematis Society and an authority on the Montana clematis.

The Structure of the Montana Flower

The make-up of anything depends on the use that is going to be made of it. In the case of a clematis flower its use is to make sure that there will be more clematis plants, otherwise clematis will disappear. To ensure the continuation of the human race, a male cell is required to come into contact with a female cell. This in turn forms a seed which, when planted into the womb of the female, will ultimately develop into another human being. It is exactly the same in the clematis plant. We need a male cell, pollen grain (in the stamen) to meet a female cell (in the carpel). The two have to come together and make a seed that the wind will carry to plant in the ground and make a new clematis.

In clematis we also need something to carry the male cell (pollen grain) from the stamen to the female cell in the carpel. This can be done by the wind or by insects, attracted by colourful petals, who come to feed on the pollen. The pollen from that clematis, or another they have visited, clings to their bodies and these clinging cells may touch the sticky tip of the carpel when it is immediately pounced upon. The pollen travels down the carpel and meets the female cell. The two cells come together in the carpel to make an embryo which becomes a seed.

So we need 1) petals to attract the insects; 2) stamens to supply male cells; 3) a pistil of carpels to supply female cells. We can think of these three parts as circles. A clematis flower may take many shapes but will always have three circles (See Plate 6).

The parts of a montana flower are seen diagramatically below.
1. The outer circle of four pink tepals.
2. The middle circle of yellow stamens
3. The inner circle of green carpels.

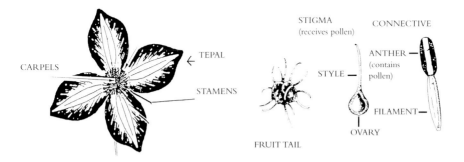

CARPEL (female reproductive part)
Stigma	receives and nurtures pollen
Style	stem of ovary
Ovary	produces seed
Fruit tails	showy tail to the seed

STAMEN (male reproductive part)
Anthur	contains pollen
Connective	area between anthers
Filament	stalk of stamen

Figure III
The parts of a montana flower in diagram form.(See also Plate 6)

PLATE 6.
'Mayleen'.

We can now dissect a montana flower to have a closer look at the three circles of its structure.

CIRCLE 1 – Circle of tepals – the outside circle.

I have chosen, for study, the attractive flower of 'Mayleen'. Please take from your garden just one flower from a montana plant and do what I do. (If the montanas are not in flower take a flat flower from any other group.)

Most flowers have a green sepal that protects the flower and a petal that attracts insects. Clematis flowers are different in that the sepal does two jobs. It protects the flower like a sepal and attracts the insects with bright colours – like a petal. So it is given a special name – 'tepal'. This is true of all clematis. In the outside circle as you can see are four pink tepals. (Plate 7)
Your flower will also have a ring of colourful tepals.

PLATE 7.
Four pink tepals at side view.

PLATE 8.
Now a circle of short thin stems – the stamens – can be seen.

CIRCLE 2 – Circle of Stamens – the middle circle.

I have removed two tepals from the flower facing the camera. **If you prefer you can take off all the tepals from your flower.** We can now see inside the flower. (See Plate 8.)

There are two parts to each stamen.
1.   The long lower part is called the filament – white here.
2.   The anthers at the top – yellow here.
The important part is the anther for it produces many, male cells – the pollen grain.

Having taken the tepals away in your flower you will see the stamens. Pluck one stamen out, put it on a dark coloured paper, and you will soon see its two parts.

23

CIRCLE 3 – The pistil – the inside circle.

I have now removed all of the stamens facing the camera. **You can remove some or all the stamens in your flower.** We can now see the pistil which consists of the tight circle of carpels at the very centre of the flower. There are a number of them, ten or more. They are tightly packed together.and each is a silky green. (See Plate 9.)

PLATE 9.
The pistil, made up of a number of carpels, is in the centre of the flower.

A pollen grain sticks to the stigma. Once a pollen grain is accepted, the door shuts and no more grains can enter.

The male cell slips down the stalk, (the style) of the carpel, meets the female cell in the ovary and in time forms a seed. Each flower can produce a number of seeds as there are a number of carpels. The seeds will float away on the wind, find soil, root, and so we have more clematis flowers. **You can take one carpel out of the bunch and you will see the tiny, sticky stigma at the very top.**

For us, clematis are grown for their attractive shape, colour and scent. For the flowers, the serious business of making seeds is now over – and so they die. We humans likewise, though we do try to achieve rather more than merely making seeds!

The Life of the Montana Flower

The montana flower is a source of beauty to the gardener but its actual function, of course, is for reproduction. Colour and shade are there to attract and serve the insects that undertake the essential task of bringing the male and female parts of the plant together. The pollen must travel from the male anther, to the tip of the female carpel, the stigma, from where it travels to the ovary. A seed results which has the capacity to reproduce the plant. Below are described and illustrated the stages in the life of the montana flower, 'Freda'.

STAGE I **Bud.**
Tepals protect the interior of flower.
Four tepals touch at edges (valvate).

See Plate 10.

STAGE II **Bud opening.**
Deep red colour of four tepals.
Between tepals and carpels a tight group of yellow stamens.
Tight group of green carpels in centre.

See Plate 11.

STAGE III **Early flower.**
Four tepals fully spread out and centre of each starting to fade.
Tight group of yellow stamens beginning to loosen.
Tight group of green carpels at centre.

See Plate 12.

STAGE IV **Mature flower.**
Tepals now faded to a pale pink.
Stamens are spreading out and some lie on tepals.
Yellow anther of stamen and its white stalk (filament) can be seen.
Tight group of green carpels at centre.

See Plate 13.

STAGE V **Late flower.**
Some tepals dropped off.
Stamens beginning to drop off.
Fading in carpels.

See Plate 14.

STAGE VI **Early stalk.**
Tepals gone.
Stamens dropping off.
Carpels more conspicuous.

See Plate 15.

STAGE VII **Late stalk.**
Stamens dropping off.
Styles elongating.

See Plate 16.

STAGE VIII **Very late stalk.**
Stamens and tepals gone.
Styles elongating.

See Plate 17.

STAGE IX   **Seeds forming.**
Green seeds visible.
Seed tails lengthen.

See Plate 18.

STAGE X   **Seeds forming.**
Tails become fluffy.

See Plate 19.

STAGE XI   **Seeds leaving.**
Seed with fluffy tails leave to be carried by wind.

See Plate 20.

STAGE XII   **Seeds gone.**
Receptacle which supported the flower only part left.
Receptacle will dry up and disintegrate.
Flower fulfilled its task of reproducing itself.

See Plate 21.

10

11

12

13

14

15

16

17

18

19

20

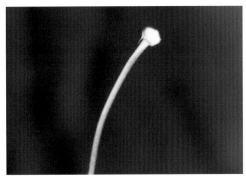
21

CHAPTER II
THE FINDING OF *CLEMATIS MONTANA*

PROLOGUE

In the early literature *Clematis montana* is followed by the appellation 'Buch-Ham' implying that its finding should be credited to this person.

Recent horticultural literature contains the information that 'Clematis montana was introduced to Europe by Countess Amhurst in 1831'.

Faced with these contradictory claims the author researched the area of the two claims and the results are reported here.

THE OLDEST CLAIM

This rests firmly on two herbaria specimens. The first in the herbarium of the Linnean Society was found at Chitlong, Nepal, on 11 April 1802. The second in the herbarium of the Natural History Museum is marked as found at Chitlong, Nepal, on 13 April 1802. They are both credited to Francis Hamilton. How did he come to be collecting in Nepal in 1802?

The Expedition

In April, 1802, a military mission crossed the border from India to Nepal. It was led by a Captain Knox. In his party was someone of great interest to us – a Francis Buchanan, M.D. (later known as Francis Hamilton).

Why was this expedition to Nepal being mounted? In 1793 the British East India Company successfully mediated between Nepalese and Chinese forces. From the better relations came a treaty in October 1801 which allowed the mission headed by Captain Knox to proceed to Khatmandu. It was a brief sojourn. The increasing hostility of the Nepalese and the insistence of Buchanan that he must leave, led to the withdrawal of the Knox mission in April 1803. But information gathered was invaluable to the British force whose intervention in 1816 led to the establishment of a permanent British residence in Khatmandu.

The Collector

Francis Buchanan, 40 years old, was an assistant surgeon, under the Superintendent, William Roxburgh, (1751–1815), at the Calcutta Botanic Garden. Buchanan was a very experienced collector, having collected plants in Mysore and Burma. He was accompanied to Nepal by an Indian artist. He was also accompanied by Indian staff collectors. 'whom I employed to obtain information so far as I prudently could'. (*An Account of the Kingdom of Nepal*. Francis Hamilton. Edinburgh. 1819.) The Nepalese were suspicious of the venture as can be seen from an extract of a letter from Buchanan to Roxburgh:

'I spoke to Captain Knox on the subject who informed me that very serious objections have been made by the Nepal government to the number of Europeans now in company with him although they are only the usual number attached to the number of troops composing the escort; and that the strongest objections would be made to the coming of any person who had no evident employment but that of spying the nakedness of the land.'

The Collection

Buchanan travelled to the Nepalese border by first taking a boat up the Ganges to Patna. He was later to write a book *An Account of the Fishes found in the River Ganges and its Branches.* (Francis Hamilton. Edinburgh. 1819.) Thereafter he travelled on foot. There was a wait in India while the party collected itself. Buchanan was impatient of the delay, but on 18 March 1802, they crossed the company's boundary near the Bena River and set off for Gar Pasana, and onwards to cross the mountains.

'We have made our entry into the dominions of Nepal and were received near the frontier by many of the principal men of the country with the greatest civility and attention. We have halted after advancing about two miles and political arrangements have occasioned a long delay but it is expected that every thing will be adjusted by the 5th and that then we shall proceed towards the capital'.

On 11 April the party stopped near Chitlong overlooking the Valley of Khatmandu and only eleven miles from Khatmandu. Ever observant Buchanan registered the temperature here and found it to be 58°F (14°C). The winters were never severe. He also heard the familiar note of the cuckoo. He was not impressed with the Nepalese Valleys: 'In sight of Katmandu in a large bare ugly valley resembling many of those of Scotland before the introduction of fences or other improvements', nor the Nepalese people: 'I wish the people were like those of Europe'.

It was here near Chitlong on 11 April 1802 that Buchanan found Clematis montana, the most exciting of all his many findings. We can share his excitement. One of his collectors would draw his attention to a large flowered plant climbing into a tree. (Plate 1) We know from his herbarium specimens that it was in bloom. As he approaches he can see the small white open flowers. (Plate 2) Approaching closer he would note the flowers' fragrance. (Plate 3) Closer still and he can study the detail of *Clematis montana* for the first time. (Plate 4) Behind the flower he would see the leaf of ternate leaflets, the hallmark of this group.(Plate 5) But his greatest interest would be to see if there was viable seed. There was. (Plate 6) This vital discovery led to a plant being in bloom in the garden of the Horticultural Society in London in less than ten years. More plants were collected on 13 April.

Buchanan was in the habit during his travel to Katmandu to send a letter and a package of plants, approximately once a day to Roxburgh at the Calcutta Botanic Gardens. The author has studied his letters. The letter written on 12 April discloses a hazard. He mentions the parcel number 8 sent on 11 April, the ninth parcel on this day, 12 April, and the tenth to be sent on 13 April. *C. montana* was found on 11 and 13 April The tenth parcel never reached Calcutta. Checking the lists of plants in the letters the author found that the montana specimens would have been in the tenth parcel. *C. montana* was not in the eighth, ninth or eleventh parcels. Although the tenth parcel was lost, we have to assume that Buchanan, prudently, took duplicate specimens with him to Khatmandu.

Francis Buchanan made good use of his time in Nepal. Nepal is 500 miles long and 150 miles at its widest. It includes one third of the Himalayan mountain chain. Buchanan formed a herbarium of between 1500–2000 specimens, many drawings and had sent 117 consignments of plants, herbarium specimens and seeds, etc., to the developing Calcutta Botanic Garden. Only twenty-one were lost.

PLATE 22.
C. montana from a distamce.

PLATE 23.
A closer look at a *C. montana*.

Calcutta

The Calcutta Botanic Garden, where Buchanan sent his plants to the Superintendent, Dr Roxburgh, was founded in Calcutta, the city that was to become the centre of British India. Its Chief Judge, Sir William Jones, was sometimes known as 'Persian Jones' for his fluency in the Persian language; having founded an Asian Society, and a museum, he went on to found, in 1786, a Botanic Garden under the management of Colonel Robert Kyd. This was to become one of the finest botanic gardens in the world. In 1789 William Roxburgh (1751–1815) who had trained in medicine at Edinburgh, became Superintendent. Despite severe migraine, Roxburgh was an energetic manager and had a strenuous family life with three marriages and at least fifteen children. Buchanan worked for and under Roxburgh, who fully supported him though the younger man was no admirer of the senior; his grasp of Latin displeased him. Roxburgh's masterpiece was his *Flora Indica*, published in four volumes after his death.

More of Francis Buchanan

We know a great deal about Buchanan. Francis Buchanan (1762-1829) was born at Branziet, Callander, Scotland in 1762 and undertook medical training at Edinburgh, where a fellow student was James Edward Smith, a key figure in our narrative. After being a ship's surgeon for long voyages that included China and the Philippines, he became an assistant surgeon for the East India Company and was posted to Burma in 1794. He built up a large collection of Burmese plants. After posts in Bengal and the study of fish, he was selected to undertake a massive brief in 1800 – a survey of Mysore – published in three volumes in 1807. Appointed to accompany Captain Knox to Katmandu, he was described by Roxburgh as 'the best botanist in India'. He was said to be able, arrogant, intolerant, combative and forceful. Buchanan was in Knox's group both as physician and botanist.

On his return from Nepal in 1803 Buchanan became personal physician to the Governor-General, Lord Wellesley (brother of the Duke of Wellington). He accompanied the Governor-General to England in 1805. Here he gave his Nepal collection and notes to his friend J. E. Smith. He was to regret this later as deprived of these, he was unable to engage in the study of Indian botany. He met Lord Minto as a fellow member of the Royal Society and returned with him to India when the latter became Governor-General in 1807. He then undertook a massive survey of Bengal and running a new society – the Institution for Promoting Natural History of India. Roxburgh departed due to ill health in 1813 and proposed his son William as Superintendent of the Botanic Garden. However, Sir Joseph Banks gave decisive support to Buchanan who became Superintendent of Calcutta Botanic Garden but he, partly due to ill health, had lost interest in remaining in India – despite coveting this post above all others. After less than four months, in February 1815, he handed over the garden to Nathaniel Wallich and returned to England by 1816, never to return to India.

There was, however, an acrimonious exchange with the new Governor-General, Lord Moira, over ownership of Buchanan's manuscripts. The latter were returned to London but the East India Company would not release them to him. Writing to Wallich in 1817, he commented as follows: '…the Court of Directors has indeed received my collection with such contempt and arrogance that I would neither ask nor receive any favour from so scoundrelly a body!' His discontent found its way into his correspondence with Wallich, in which he advised '…do not throw your pearls before swine but collect largely and keep your collections for the learned of your own

PLATE 24.
A small group of flowers of *C. montana.*

PLATE 25.
A close look at a single bloom of *C. montana*.

country (Denmark) who I have no doubt would be thankful.' He also wrote
'…my advice to you as an old man of a good deal of experience in India and
Europe, is along with your search after science, to collect money as fast as
possible, and whenever you have a competence to return to your native country.'

In a letter to his friend, J. E. Smith, from India in 1797, Buchanan had
revealed that his ambition was to take a wife and collect £6,000 – so that he
could buy books. Both ambitions were attained. He married soon after his
return to Scotland and unexpected wealth came his way. His mother
inherited three estates, Bardowie, Spittal and Leny, and by the terms of the
entail assumed the name of Hamilton. Her eldest son died. Her second son,
Colonel John Hamilton, became her heir and changed his name to
Hamilton. But he died. His son, Francis, Buchanan's nephew, would have
been heir – but he had already died. Francis now came into the inheritance
in 1818 and but had to change his name to Hamilton.

Most of his life he had been Buchanan. Most of his publications were in
later life under his name Hamilton. Sometimes he was referred to as
Hamilton Buchanan, and at other times as Buchanan Hamilton. (He was
Chief of the Buchanans of Buchanan.) Others refer to his early work under
'Buchanan' and later work under 'Hamilton'. Often the abbreviated 'Buch-
Ham' is used for his botanical work. Others have used the abbreviation 'B-
Ham'. He has also had the appellation Francis Hamilton (né Buchanan).

After settling in Scotland he took an active interest in botany, in the Royal
Society of which he was a Fellow, and in the Linnean Society of which he
was also a Fellow. He settled first at Callander, near Stirling, and later at Leny.

His area had a climate 'worse than India'. He wrote two books *An Account of the Kingdom of Nepal*, 1819, and *An Account of the Fishes Found in the River Ganges and its Branches*, 1819. He died at Leny, Scotland, on 15 June 1829, aged sixty-seven.

The Fate of Buchanan's Specimens

C. montana, as we have seen, was collected 11 and 13 April 1802 and we need to follow what happened to it and the rest of his collection. In 1805 Buchanan returned to England. This would have necessitated the long and hazardous journey round the Cape of Good Hope. Not only a journey hazardous to people but also to plants. The Wardian Case was yet to be invented. Herbarium specimens and seeds readily survived but not living plants. Robert Fortune, the celebrated clematis collector, some 50 years later, was to revolutionise the Indian economy by bringing the live tea plants from China to Calcutta using Wardian cases.

In London in 1805 Buchanan met with two key people, A. B. Lambert and J .E. Smith. In common they had wealth and an urge to collect plants in their herbaria. Both wished to build up national collections. One was to succeed, the other's collection disintegrated.

James Edward Smith (1759–1828) came from a wealthy Norwich wool family. He trained in medicine at Edinburgh (where he was a contemporary and friend of Buchanan) Leyden, and London. He then devoted himself entirely to the study of plants. He was a friend of Sir Joseph Banks, (1743–1820), who also had a large herbarium. Linnaeus had died. His son inherited his collections. He died a bachelor. He elected not to marry as one lady he admired had not had smallpox, might be stricken with it and be disfigured. His other admired lady had already been disfigured. His property, including his father's collections, were left to his mother and sister. They were desirous of obtaining 1,000 guineas (a guinea being one pound and one shilling) for his herbarium and library. They had their eyes on the distinguished Sir Joseph Banks but he declined. However, he drew the offer to

PLATE 26.
The ternate leaf of *C. montana.*

PLATE 27.
The seeds of *C. montana*.

the attention of the young J. E. Smith (later Sir James Smith). With the help of a loan from his father, he accepted. The matter had to be dealt with quickly as the King of Sweden was away travelling. The ladies suspected that the King on his return would press for the material to go to Uppsala University and probably at a much reduced sum. So it proved. On his return an angry king sent a ship to intercept the vessel carrying the material to London. But in vain. In 1784 , the material found its way safely to J. E. Smith who had plans for founding a botanical society. In due course he founded the Linnean Society in 1788 and, on his death, the Linnean material was acquired by public subscription for the new society, where it still resides. He was its first president. A. B. Lambert was a vice-president.

It was to J.E. Smith that Buchanan gave his original collection and papers on his return in 1805. He gave them personally to Smith. He hoped that Smith would use the material in publications and bringing credit to Smith and Buchanan. Unfortunately Smith made almost no use of them. Buchanan spoke of him as 'indolent'. Smith later, as was his right, gave the material to the Linnean Society. Buchanan was to regret his generosity as he had no ready access to his material, 'Smith has it all'. The 'all' consisted of 1,500 specimens of which 700-800 were new, 114 drawings, and his manuscripts. There is much to suggest that later Smith was very active with a considerable contribution to the literature.

  Aylmer Bourke Lambert (1761-1842) was the most fortunate of men. Only son of a country gentleman whose property he would inherit, he also inherited a large fortune from his mother. An early interest in plants developed into a passion for collecting them into his herbarium and acquiring all known books about them. His wealth allowed him to do this to his heart's content. A house in London housed his herbarium and library and kept him in touch with the distinguished botanists of his day. J. E. Smith was a personal friend and brought him into the Linnean Society as a vice-president in 1796. To add to his assets came a marriage to a charming and intelligent lady prepared to share his interests and act as his secretary when required.

After inheriting his father's residence, Boyton House, in Wiltshire in 1820 they could lead the life of a London gentleman and lady at 26 Lower Grosvenor Street or of country gentlefolk at will. A feature of his life was his generosity. He actively encouraged botanists from home and abroad to make use of his library and herbarium. Lambert's first interest was collecting which he conducted assiduously and with passion. Using his collection was a secondary interest but balanced by the use made of it by others. His main literary contribution was a book on pines, for which he had a great deal of help from others. His collections enjoyed universal praise. Described as 'one of the most valuable collections ever made by a private individual', and 'the most liberal botanist in England'. J.C. Loudon in his monumental *Encyclopaedia of Plants,* 1841, was to write '…without the herbarium of Mr Lambert … this work could not have been produced'. The great French systemiser, De Candolle, visited in 1816. At Lambert's death, aged 80, in 1842, the herbarium held 50,000 specimens from 130 collections with 1,350 titles in his library.

It would be happy to report that this state of bliss would continue. But a number of factors collectively intervened and brought this noble enterprise to a sorry end. His investments at home and abroad ceased to bring in the ample income he had enjoyed. His support, his wife, fell into a long illness and died. In 1820 an able botanist, David Don, was employed and gave assiduous service. However, Don fell out with Lambert and was dismissed in 1826 for marrying the latter's cook. Don was also librarian to the Linnean Society and subsequently became Professor of Botany at King's College, London.

Despite his benevolence Lambert was given to bouts of nervous or eccentric behaviour. De Candolle described him as 'bizarre'. The collections fell into disarray as he struggled on to the age of 80. His will left his collections to the British Museum – if funds allowed. The second option was to sell the collection to the museum although they declined to buy. The third option was to sell the collections. Cruelly the last option had to be applied in June, 1842 and this led to their dispersal.

What was to happen to *C. montana* in these circumstances? Very good fortune it can be reported. As has been said, when Buchanan returned to England in 1805 he gave his collections and manuscripts (largely from Nepal and Mysore) to J. E. Smith. In due course Smith gave them to the Linnean Society and there they reside to this day. From the collection is reproduced (Plate 28) the clematis found on 11 April 1802, at Chitlong and marked on the bottom left-hand corner *Clematis montana*, 'Chitlong 11th April 1802 Napaul', 'Dr F. Buchanan'.

PLATE 28.
Herbarium specimen of *C. montana* found by Dr F. Buchanan. From the Herbarium of the Linnean Society.

PLATE 29.
Herbarium specimen of *C. montana* found 13
April 1802 by Dr F. Buchanan and from the
Herbarium of the Natural History Museum.

Buchanan gave his duplicates to A. B.
Lambert. These included the specimen
collected on 13 April 1802. Lambert's
collections were split up into 317 lots
when they went on sale. The lot
containing *C. montana*, Lot 286, was bought
for £9 for the British Museum by Robert
Brown (1773–1858), Keeper of their
collection, and it now resides in the
herbarium of the Natural History Museum.
Reproduced here is (Plate 29) a photocopy
of the top part of the *C. montana* collected
by Buchanan at Chitlong on 13 April 1802
– as marked on the specimen – 'Clematis
Montana B'; 'Chitlong 13th April 1802';
'Napaul'; 'Dr. Buchanan'.

As Loudon reports in his *Arboretum et
Fruticeum Britannicum*, 1838, Vol. I, page 245,
seed was given by Buchanan to the
Horticultural Society (now the R.H.S.) and
a plant bloomed 'soon after' in its garden.
Loudon does not make it clear whether
'soon after' refers to Buchanan's return in
1805 or De Candolle's visit in 1816. In
either event it bloomed before 1820. De
Candolle saw the plant at Lambert's
collection. He published a description in
his *Systema* of 1817. He named it 'C. montana' and established that name. David
Don, who supervised Lambert's collections from 1820–1826, in 1825 published
his *Prodramus Florae Nepalensis* based on Lambert's collections. It included *C.
anenomeflora*, his name for *C. montana*. In 1821 it was collected by N. Wallich in
Nepal – his specimen is in the Wallich Collection at Kew (No. 4681). It was
also collected by Dr. Robert Blinkworth at Kamaon north India in 1824. (No.
4681 in the same collection.)

The Newest Claim

This usually states '*C. montana* was collected in India by Lady Amherst and
brought to Europe in 1831'. This statement gets credence from a number of
respected authorities. W. J. Bean in *Trees and Shrubs hardy in the British Isles, 1914*,
states '…introduced by Lady Amherst in 1831'; Alfred Rehder's *Manual of
Cultivated Trees and Shrubs*, 1927, 'introduced in 1831'; Magnus Johnson, 2001, *The
Genus Clematis* '1831 *Clematis montana* brought from India to England by Lady
Amherst, wife of Earl Amherst who was a Governor-General of India'. To
explore this claim we need an introduction to Countess and Earl Amherst.

Countess Amherst

Countess Amherst (1762–1838) was the daughter of Lord Archer, Baron Umberslade. He, at one point, was made Governor-General of Canada but never went to Canada. However, he gave the name of 'Montreal' to his estate in Kent. Sarah Archer first married the 5th Earl of Plymouth. After his death in 1799 she married Earl Amherst in 1800 when aged 38. Our research may have the advantage of reminding us of the contributions of the resilient Countess Amherst, who died in 1838 at the age of 75. Nathaniel Wallich, distinguished Curator of the Calcutta Botanic Garden had this to say of her: 'Right Honourable Countess Amherst and her daughter, Lady Alicia Amherst, the zealous friends and constant promoters of all branches of natural history, especially botany'. In botany the magnificent tree 'Amherstia nobilis' with spectacular pendulant racemes of vermilion flowers (Plate 30) was named after mother and daughter. In zoology she is remembered by the beautiful Amherst pheasants she brought to England.

Earl Amherst

Earl Amherst had two distinguished appointments in his life. In 1816 he was appointed Ambassador to China. He and his staff left London on February 1816, travelled via Rio de Janeiro, Cape of Good Hope, Java, Hong Kong to the summer palace of the Emperor, six miles north west of Peking. He was accompanied by a Dr Clarke Abel who later became his personal physician in India. His mission was to represent to the Emperor the wrongs suffered by British subjects. Misfortune then occurs – 28 August 1816 – 'Ambassador urged to enter the Royal Presence and to prostrate, refuses, is insulted, quits the palace'. The Ambassador starts his journey home the same day and returns via Nanking, Canton and Manila. They reached St. Helena on 27t June and the Ambassador had an interview with the Emperor Napoleon. It is not clear who interviewed whom. It went well and we must assume that prostration was not required. They reached Portsmouth on 15 August 1817. The expedition had taken eighteen months owing to the slowness of travel at that time. The only beneficiary was Dr Clarke Abel who collected a great many plants but lost them in a shipwreck of the warship taking them back to England.

In 1823 Earl Amherst's second appointment was that of Governor-General of India with the Government based in Calcutta. This time he was accompanied by his wife Sarah, daughter Alicia, and son Jeffery (they had five children.) Countess Sarah was now aged 61. The Earl was to have a torrid time due to the aggression of the King of Burma. On the defeat of the latter, things were less troubled and he felt free to embark on a procession in August 1826, through the Northern Provinces – wild and largely unknown. Most unhappily, however, and before their departure, both the Earl and his son were struck down by what was probably cholera. Jeffery died.

PLATE 30.
'Amherstia nobilis'.

The Collecting

It took eight long months for Lord Amherst's party to get to Simla, which they reached in April 1827, a good time for collecting *Clematis montana*. Their personal physician, Dr Clarke Abel, died on the way, at Cawnpore (Kanpur). Simla was undeveloped and consisted of just one European house. However, after the plains it must have been a refreshing stay which lasted ten weeks. It was during this period that the mother and daughter Alicia, plant collected avidly. It was also during this period that they found *Clematis montana* – no doubt experiencing Buchanan's excitement. Some seeds were sent home there and then, but the main collection accompanied their return journey in 1828 (not 1831 as is commonly stated).

The party left Calcutta for home in March 1828 and reached Portsmouth on 22 July 1828, a four-month hazardous journey. They returned to Montreal, Kent, the seat of the father of Countess Sarah. It was in the garden of this house that she grew *C. montana* from seed. She was to present 'flowering specimens' to David Don in May, 1834, six years after returning home. Don described the plant in *The British Flower Garden* by Robert Sweet in May, 1885. In the same publication Don also records that ' ...the species was originally collected by Dr Francis Hamilton, at Chitlong, in the Valley of Nepal'.

The facts are unequivocal. Countess Amherst found *C. montana* in Simla in 1827, twenty-five years after Buchanan found it in Nepal and brought *C. montana* back to Europe in 1828 (not 1831), twenty-three years after Buchanan brought it back in 1805. All this is thoroughly recorded at the time. Where, therefore, was the origin of the false information?

Exploring the Claim

To track down the source of the error it was necessary to survey the literature of botany, and in particular that of Indian plants, from 1805 to the present. The reader will be spared the detail but will receive salient material.

Buchanan gave his material to J. E. Smith and A. B. Lambert in 1805 and we have the specimens today. J. C. Loudon records 'from specimens derived from him (Buchanan) it was first described by De Candolle in his 1817 Systema' (Systema. Vol.I. p.164.). The record was repeated in De Candolle's Prod.Vol.I. p.9. 1823). David Don, by now Professor of Botany at King's College, London, had handled the specimens as Lambert's assistant and describes it as *C. anemoniflora* in *Prodromus Florae Nepalensis*, p.197. 1825. ('A Preliminary Description of the Flora of Nepal' 1825.) and states ' ... found in vicinity of Chitlong, Nepariae by Hamilton'. (Nepal [Nepariae] was spelt in a variety of ways. By now Buchanan was named 'Hamilton'.)

George Don, David Don's brother, in *A General System of Gardening and Botany*, 1831.Vol.I. p.9, refers to Hamilton's manuscript and adds, ' ...native of Nepaul, in the vicinity of Chitlong'. Nathaniel Wallich included *C. montana* in his *Plantae Asiaticae Rariones*. As shown in Plate 14, done in the new lithographic process, and Table 217, he credits the plant to Hamilton. David Don

Figure IV.
Figures reproduced by Loudon in his *Arboretum et Fruticetum Britannicum* (1838). The upper figure is of the plant in the Horticultural Society garden and the lower is of the plant at Montreal, Kent. (This reproduction, from an old book, does not give ideal results but is justified by its historic significance.)

was Editor of Robert Sweet's *The British Flower Garden*. 1835. Table 253. II. 5. This is the first mention of the Countess Sarah introduction. He states, ' ...flowering specimens were originally communicated to us in May last (May 1834) by Lady Sarah Amherst, from Montreal, Kent, the seat of her noble father'. He makes clear that this was not the first finding, ' ...the species was originally collected by Dr Francis Hamilton, at Chitlong, in the Valley of Nepal ...'.

The early literature is correct but two years later the first error crept in. J. C. Loudon in the *Gardeners' Magazine* 1837, p.20 was to state, 'Introduced from the Himalayas by Lady Amherst'. Loudon immediately corrected himself and gave a detailed account of the findings by Buchanan and Lady Amherst. This was in *Arboretum et Fruticetum Britannicum* (*The Trees and Shrubs of Britain*) Vol.1. 1838. p.245. He states, ' ...Dr Buchanan originally collected specimens of this species at Chitong in the Valley of Nepal' and 'Plants soon afterwards raised from seeds in the garden of the London Horticultural Society...' (now Royal Horticultural Society). He added two figures – one of the original plant at the Horticultural Society (Figure IV) and that of the plant at Montreal, Kent (Figure IV).

Figure IV.

The error soon recurred. John Lindley in the *Botanical Register*, 1840. Vol. 23. Table 53, says that *C. montana* was brought from India by Lady Amherst. B. Maund (1790-1863), who was Editor of a thirteen volume *Botanic Garden 1825–1851*, describes *C. montana* in a late volume. Having correctly described the plant he makes two questionable statements – 'from Nepa in 1831?' and 'This species was brought from India, by the late Lady Amherst'. This is the first mention of the year and although he questions the date this became unquestioned in the errors later.

The *Botanical Magazine*, 1844. No.4061, gave a detailed description of *C. montana* var. *grandiflora* and in the course of it mentions its history in detail. The article states that 'Dr. Buchanan collected it at Chitlong in the Valley of Nepal'. Subsequently all the Indian botanical literature and the general literature in England and the Continent was to give the correct information. Partial errors crept in – Moore & Jackman's *The Clematis As A Garden Flower* 1877 state that '*C. grata* and *C. montana* were introduced in 1831' and this is repeated in C. Nicholson's *Illustrated Dictionary of Gardening* 1885 'Nepaul 1831'.

But now we come to the crucial error. W. J. Bean in *The Garden*, 25 December 1897, was to say that *C. montana* – ' ...was first brought to Britain by Lady Amherst in 1831'. This error found its way into his influential reference work *Trees and Shrubs Hardy in the British Isles*. 1914. Thus we are not surprised to read (J.R.H.S.) when *C. montana* was awarded its Award of Garden Merit in 1930, that ' ...in 1831 Lady Amherst introduced to England...' It was repeated in Ernest Markham's *Clematis* in 1935, in Stanley B. Whitehead's

Garden Clematis in 1959, and in all clematis books subsequently. A small error in Bean's magnificent work became thereafter a part of the lore of clematis. In the dawning days of horticulture it is fair to say that it was no disadvantage for a plant to be associated with the nobility.

Epilogue

We can record the facts. *Clematis montana* was first collected by Dr Francis Buchanan near Chitlong, Nepal, on 11 April 1802. It was collected by Dr Wallich in Nepal in 1821 and by Dr Blinkworth in North India in 1824. It was also collected by Countess Sarah Amherst and daughter Alicia in Simla in 1827. Buchanan introduced it to England in 1805. It was soon in flower in the garden of The Horticultural Society of London. It was described in publications in Paris in 1818 and London in 1825.

Turning from our cherished flower, our quest brings admiration for these early collectors – the exacting Dr Buchanan and the intrepid Amherst ladies. They quested in dangerous uncomfortable regions far from home, moved by a drive that we still share today.

Chapter III

The Montanas Described

In this chapter members of the group and related sub-groups are introduced and presented in alphabetical order. But *Clematis montana* the first collected, and which gave the group its name, is taken first.

The one page description of each plant has four sections.

I   There is a general description of the plant and its merits.

II   Technical data given for each plant together with any Award of Garden Merit (AGM) of the Royal Horticultural Society of the United Kingdom.

III   Photographs of each montana.

IV   Consideration of a montana may stimulate points of interest – intriguing facts, episodes, connections or historical links; a submission is made for each flower.

A SECTION 'IDENTIFYING YOUR CLEMATIS' IS THEN DEVOTED TO NOTES AND PLATES TO ASSIST IDENTIFICATION OF THE PLANTS.

PLATE 31.
Clematis montana (syn. *C. montana* 'Alba').

Clematis montana (syn. *C. montana* 'Alba')

This the first montana to be introduced and it immediately established the outstanding features of the group to which it gave its name – huge size of plant, its floriferous nature, and its immense vigour. The small open flowers are white and produced in great profusion – covering the plant. It is also fragrant. Give it plenty of room for dramatic effect. Wonderful up large trees.

Name:	This stands for 'of the mountain'.
Origin:	Collected by Francis Buchanan (later became Francis Hamilton) in Chitlong, Nepal, on 11 April 1802. Introduced to Europe via England by Francis Buchanan in 1805. Also collected by Nathaniel Wallich in Nepal in 1821, by Dr Robert Blinkworth in Northern India in 1824, and Countess Amherst at Simla, Northern India, in 1827.
Habit:	Deciduous climber; very vigorous; profuse flowerer; height – up to 12m. (40ft.).
Flower:	Single open flower, up to 6 cm. (2¼ in.) across, on long thin light-green stalks; clear white colour with trace of pink at back of tepal; four broad-elliptic tepals with no overlap; anthers are yellow with white or greeny-white filament; pistil is silky green; produced in clusters from leaf axils, occasionally single; fragrant – likened to pinks or carnations.
Foliage:	Ternate; oblong pointed incised leaflets; light-green; slightly bronze young leaves.
Special Features:	Extensively grown. Compare with 'Grandiflora' which has larger flower. Distinctive features are the small star-shaped scented white flowers produced in profusion on a large plant. AGM 1930, withdrawn 2002.

PLATE 32.
Clematis montana.

Buchanan, Hamilton, or Buch-Ham?

When he collected his plants, including *Clematis montana*, in India the collector was known as 'Buchanan'. But in 1818, by the terms of the entail of the estates he inherited, Buchanan had to change his name to 'Hamilton'. This has led to problems in referring to him. 'Buchanan' is correct when he collected. 'Hamilton' is correct when he wrote his books and papers after 1818. Generally, experts call him 'Hamilton'. Others call him 'Buchanan-Hamilton' or 'Hamilton-Buchanan'. In botanical works the abbreviation 'Buch-Ham' is usually employed – which always provokes a question mark.

PLATE 33.
Prolific flowering of *Clematis montana.*

PLATE 34.
A close-up of the flower of 'Alexander'.

'Alexander'

To have a bloom larger than *C. montana* and to have strong fragrance should give a plant a fine recommendation. Unhappily the plant is slow to establish – even taking some years to do so. Once established it makes a fine vigorous plant.

Name:	After its collector Colonel R. D. Alexander.
Origin:	Found in North India by Colonel R. D. Alexander and introduced by Jim Fisk, Westleton, Suffolk, U.K., in 1961.
Habit:	Deciduous climber; vigorous to 6m. (20ft.); not as profuse a flowerer as some montanas.
Flowers:	Creamy-green bud; single and often opens as a slightly 'cupped' flower; cream at first moving to creamy-white; 'crinkley' edge to tepals; yellow anthers; green connective; filament greeny-white; pistil – green and prominent; up to 8cm. (3¼in.) across; strong sweet fragrance; flowers early for the group.
Foliage:	Mid-green and larger than *C. montana*; broken edges; bronze young leaves.
Special Features:	Flowers distinguished by scent, 'cupped' nature of early flower, 'crinkly' edge to tepals and creamy white colour.

PLATE 35.
The flowers of 'Alexander'.

A Near Thing

Buchanan on his journey to Khatmandu was in the habit of sending a package of the collected plant material with an accompanying letter and list each day to his superior, Dr Roxburgh, at the Botanic Garden, Calcutta. During his stay in Nepal he sent 117 consignments. 21 were lost. *C. montana* should have been in the tenth consignment but this was lost. Buchanan prudently kept reserves. In due course *C. montana* came to Calcutta with Buchanan and onwards via the Cape of Good Hope to England, to J.E. Smith's herbarium and later to the herbarium of the Linnean Society, where it resides today.

PLATE 36.
'Alexander'– the leaf form.

49

PLATE 37.
'Broughton Star'- a fine double clematis.

'Broughton Star'

This is a fine double clematis – probably the finest – depending on your taste. There are two rings of tepals. The inner, truly pistillodes, are dark purple-red and harmonise well with the outer ring of lighter purple-pink to make an attractive flower. Vigorous and flowers profusely. Can flower into early summer. An outstanding plant.

Name:	Signifies place of hybridising – Broughton, Lancashire, U.K.
Origin:	A cross of 'Marjorie' and 'Picton's Variety'. Created by Vince and Sylvia Denny at Broughton, Lancashire, U.K. and introduced in 1988.
Habit:	A deciduous climber. Grows up to 5m. (18ft.). Very floriferous with dense covering of flowers. Vigorous.
Flowers:	Double usually and occasionally semi-double. Up to 6.5cm. (2½in.) across. Inner ring of purple-red pistillodes – up to 14 in number and narrow – elliptical and pointed; outer ring of four tepals is lighter purple-pink; flowers in clusters, up to six in number; anthers – yellow; pistil is silky-green turning to yellow. My plants have failed to yield scent.
Foliage:	Small ternate leaves – dark-green but sometimes bronzed. Broken edges.
Special Features:	Distinctive for its colour and double flower. British Clematis Society's Certificate of Merit, 1998. AGM – 2002.

Who were the Collectors?

In general, plants have been collected by two groups of people. The first group were part-timers. Doctors, like Buchanan and Abel had medical duties as their main task but collected in any spare time. Missionaries such as David and Delavey were a similar group. Dr Henry was a customs officer in China and started collecting, he said, out of boredom.

PLATE 38.
'Broughton Star'.

PLATE 39.
A distant view of 'Broughton Star'.

The other group were full-timers such collectors as E. H. Wilson and Robert Fortune. These had a background in horticulture or botany and were supported by botanical gardens, societies, or by their own finance. All had in common a link with a herbarium in their own or another country – Potanin with St. Petersburgh, Henry with Kew, E. H. Wilson with Arnold Arboretum. The link might be with a commercial company that grew and introduced their plants; E. H. Wilson with Veitch & Sons would be an example.

PLATE 40.
Clematis chrysocoma.

Clematis chrysocoma

This is a representative of a sub-group of the montanas. It makes an attractive plant for its foliage and flowers covered in parts in plentiful golden hair. It flowers after the main group of montanas. It needs a sheltered wall, south facing if possible, as it can be vulnerable to low temperatures and late frost. Vigorous and full of flowers once established. It has a longer flowering period than the montanas. Flowers are good for cutting. May have a flush of flowers in the autumn. A desirable plant.

Name:	Stands for golden (chrysos) and hair (kome).
Origin:	Original true plant collected by Père Jean Marie Delavay at Lan Kien Ho, Yunnan, China, in August 1884. He sent seed to the nursery of M. Maurice Vilmorin, Verrières le Buisson, near Versailles, France. Vilmorin introduced it to Kew in 1910. It was later discovered by George Forrest. Some seed from the wild have produced variable amounts of white and pink in the flower. In the wild it is sometimes found with satiny pink flowers on long stems. That brought back by Roy Lancaster in the 1980s was white. The true form is said to be dwarf and the plant on the market is a hybrid, probably between *C. chrysocoma* and *C. montana* 'Rubens'.
Habit:	The plant in cultivation is a deciduous climber that makes a vigorous plant up to 4.5m. (15ft.). Some forms can be 'shrubby' in habit. If cut back in a severe winter it will usually recover. May have a second crop of flowers or give sporadic flowering.

Flower:	Four tepals – wide obovate in shape, making a 'cupped' flower at first; white tinged with pinky-violet in young flowers; up to 7.5cm. (3in.) across; at back of tepal there is a violet colour around edge; anther – yellow; filament – cream; pistil – silky-green and prominent; clusters of up to eight in number on firm long stalks; hairs on stalks; no scent; amount of pink in flower is variable and is attributed to possible crossing with *C. montana* 'Rubens'.
Foliage:	Ternate, three elliptic-obovate (reverse egg-shaped) leaflets with broken edges; dense hairs on back of leaflets and stalk; dark-green.
Special Features:	Distinctive for its foliage, hairiness and 'cupped' flower. Good for cutting. Long flowering period. A.M. 1936. See Historical Notes, Chapter XI for discussion of true *C. chrysocoma*.

PLATE 41.
Clematis chrysocoma.

PLATE 42.
Leaf of *Clematis chrysocoma.*

A Missionary Collector

Intrepid and religious, Père Jean Marie Delavay (1838-1895) was one of a distinguished group of Catholic priests who took advantage of a mission in China to collect plants. Stationed in Yunnan 1882–1897, and again 1893–1895, he collected for Mr A. Franchet at the Musée d' Hist. Nat., Paris, 200,000 specimens of which 1,500 were new species and five of the latter were clematis, including *Clematis chrysocoma*. He survived an attack of plague at the end of his first visit to Yunnan. However, on the second visit, he became increasingly unwell and died in Yunnan aged 57.

PLATE 43.
'Continuity' (syn. *C. chrysocoma* 'Continuity').

'Continuity' (syn. *C. chrysocoma* 'Continuity')

This is one of the most striking, showy, clematis in the group. This is because of the hugely attractive blooms. These have long protruding stamens with a background of a green pistil. The flower is on a long firm stalk making it ideal for cutting. The flowers dance in the breeze. It needs a warm wall away from cold winds. The flowering period is long. Outstanding clematis if given right conditions.

Name:	Denotes the attempt of the plant to produce continuous flowering. A sequence of flowerings through the year with a good crop in the autumn.
Origin:	Raised by Albert Voneshan, hybridiser of Jackman's of Woking in the late 1950s and introduced by Treasures of Tenbury.
Habit:	Deciduous climber up to 4m. (13ft.). Vigorous but not hardy. Needs winter protection in cold areas and to be out of cold winds.
Flower:	This is up to 9cm. (3¾in.) across; it has four tepals that are oval with a broad wavy tip and crinkly edge; tepals fold outwards with age making an attractive shape; tepals are pinky-violet when young and mature to a pale pinky-mauve; anthers are yellow-green fading to yellow; pistil – deep-green at first fading to dark yellow; stamens up to 3cm. (1¼in.) in length; flowers cluster on long hairy stalks up to 20cm. (8in.) in length; no fragrance.

Foliage:	Mid-green with bronze tint; stalk has golden hairs.
Special	Flowers later than the main group of montanas and later
Features:	than *C. chrysocoma*.
	Attempts to make flushes of flowering throughout season with a major effort in the autumn.
	Distinctive for its late flowering, crops of flowers and gorgeous bloom dominated by long stamens.
	Good for cutting.
	Treasures of Tenbury, U.K., in 2002 claim to have a plant with white tepals.

PLATE 44.
Close-up of the flower of 'Continuity'.

Paradise

To many of us to be able to devote a lifetime to collecting specimens of plants and to have the means to buy any relevant book at will must be close to Paradise. Add to that a house, with herbarium and library, in central London and a house similarly appointed in the country. Good fortune continues with an able, amiable, wife devoted to your enterprises. Your days are enlightened by contact with the leading resident and visiting naturalists. You keep open house to all who wish to study your collections. Your generosity brings acclaim from all. Two inheritances, the first from your mother, and the second from your father, fund all your wishes. Such was the happy state of Aylmer Bourke Lambert (1761–1842).

PLATE 45.
Leaf form of 'Continuity'.

PLATE 46.
'East Malling' (syn. *C. rubens* 'E.M.F').

'East Malling' (syn. *C. rubens* 'E.M.F')

Some years ago a trial was held at a botanical research station at East Malling of clones of 'Rubens'. This variety was regarded as the best and has since been commercially available as 'Rubens E.M.F.' (East Malling Form). Judged by its vigour it is a very fine plant. However, the desirable 'Rubens' characteristics – depth of pink colour, depth of scent, bronziness of leaves are more apparent in the original 'Rubens'. It is a strong growing desirable plant.

Name:	Denotes place of trial.
Origin:	From East Malling Research Station, Kent, U.K. in 1990.
Habit:	Deciduous climber – very vigorous up to 30m (100ft). Floriferous.
Flower:	Four broad-elliptic tepals making a square flower; up to 8cm. (3in.) across; mauvy-pink throughout flower; anther – green fading to yellow; prominent green pistil turning yellow; some fragrance.
Foliage:	Ternate, large, light green.
Special Features:	Compare with 'Rubens' ; 'Rubens' has a large flower, more colour, more scent, and bronzy foliage. 'East Malling' is the more vigorous and has larger green leaves. Both are excellent plants.

Paradise Lost

A. B. Lambert's noble enterprises were to end with the saddest of all sad events – the disintegration and sale of his library, herbarium and goods. The

PLATE 47.
Close-up view of 'East Malling'.

slide to ruin probably began with the long illness and death of his able wife. His personality was not an organising one. Indeed his general demeanour was said to be 'bizarre'. His investments produced less with time. David Don, brought in to organise his collections was dismissed, for marrying his cook. Servants quarrelled. All was disarray. He still hoped that his collections would be bought and kept together by the British Museum. On his death they refused to buy. His possessions, therefore, were divided into 317 lots and sold at auction. His creditors received 5 shillings to the pound. The duplicate specimen of Buchanan's *Clematis montana* found its way to the Natural History Museum. His friend J. E. Smith had more luck with his collections. He founded the Linnean Society and they still have his collections, including Buchanan's original specimen of *C. montana*.

PLATE 48.
'East Malling' leaf form.

PLATE 49.
'East Malling' seed head.

PLATE 50.
'Elizabeth'- a close-up of the flower.

'Elizabeth'

This is a long time favourite. It scores for its vigorous nature and gorgeous scent. The fragrance of all other montanas is judged by the fragrance of 'Elizabeth'. The flowers are pale pink. It can make a very large plant. Everyone grows this one.

Name:	A popular English female Christian name and probably a member of the raiser's family.
Origin:	A chance seedling at nursery of Jackman's of Woking and listed in *Rowland Jackman's Planter's Handbook*, 1953/54.
Habit:	A deciduous climber. Very vigorous. Can climb to 8m. (20ft.). A profuse flowerer.
Flower:	There are four tepals making an open gappy flower; tepals are broad and oblanceolate (tapering more gently towards base than apex)); flower is up to 7.5cm. (3in.) across; pointed, globular, mauve-pink and white bud; flower is strong mauve-pink at opening but fades from the middle so that colour is at the edge of the mature flower (reverse in 'Pink Perfection'); anther – yellow; filament – white, pistil – green fading to yellow; flowers appear in clusters, up to six, from leaf nodes; intense scent – vanilla, sweet.
Foliage:	Ternate; mid-green; bronzy when young; small.
Special	A.G.M. 1993.
Features:	Has to be compared with pale pink 'Odorata' which has smaller flower, less scent and less colour, and with pale pink 'Pink Perfection' which has colour in centre of tepal, less colour, less perfume, more prominent pistil, and broader tepals (see also page 122).
	Distinctive as a pale pink vigorous clematis with lovely scent.

PLATE 51.
The blooms of 'Elizabeth'.

Last of the Jackmans

The Jackman Nursery was founded in 1810 at Woking, Surrey, U.K. by William Jackman. Then came George senior, George junior, Arthur George, and lastly George Rowland, born in 1902. Rowland's mother died when he was five years old and so his father's housekeeper brought him up. He differed from his predecessors by not being a hybridist. He put his interest into selection – choosing the best wherever he saw it, including any seedlings in his nursery. One of these seedlings became 'Elizabeth'. Other celebrated introductions were 'Pamela Jackman' (Alpina Group) named after his daughter, 'Barbara Dibley' (Early Large Flowered Group) named after his secretary and 'Barbara Jackman' (Early Large Flowered Group) named after his wife. Soon after the Second World War he sold his nursery and in time it became a garden centre. Rowland, the last of the Jackmans, died in 1976.

PLATE 52.
'Elizabeth'- seed head.

PLATE 53.
'Fragrant Spring'.

'Fragrant Spring'

This plant might not outshine other pink flowered clematis but it has the virtue of attractive foliage. The foliage is an unusual light bronze and sometimes the leaf margins are not dissected. It also has fragrance.

Name:	Indicates its fragrance and time of flowering.
Origin:	Selected by Proefstation voor de Boomkwekerij, Boskoop, The Netherlands, in 1992. Selected from plants brought in for the Montana trial as 'Rubens'
Habit:	Deciduous climber up to 8m. (20ft.). Vigorous. Floriferous.
Flowers:	Four tepals up to 5cm. (2in.) across; mauve-pink that fades in centre; bud – creamy-white; tepals can recurve and twist; long stamens with yellow anthers; filaments – white; green slightly prominent pistil; strong fragrance, may have flush of flowers in autumn that have deeper pink colour.
Foliage:	Ternate. Light bronze leaflets and stem, especially in young leaf. Leaflet margin may be undissected.
Special Features:	Distinctive feature of plant is its attractive bronzy foliage with unbroken edge to leaflets. Has been compared to 'Elizabeth' but this has a larger flower. Has been compared to 'Olga' but this has purple foliage.

A Sanguine Lady

Partnership to a distinguished person may leave little room for self-expression. Countess Sarah Amherst partnered two husbands, mothered five children, and yet left a legacy in contributions to botany and zoology. Her main effort came in her stay with her husband Governor-General of India 1823–1828. Aged over 60, she was active in support to the developing Calcutta Botanic Garden. Her finest moment came at the end of a harrowing journey from Calcutta to Simla. For ten weeks in Simla she and her daughter assiduously collected botanical material, including *Clematis montana*. This latter had of course already been collected by Buchanan. The material came back to England with a live Burmese pheasant, the latter to be named after her. Her botanical specimens went to the herbarium of A. B. Lambert and, on its disintegration, to the herbarium of Kew. Nathaniel Wallich named a massive Burmese tree after mother and daughter – 'Amherstia nobilis'.

PLATE 54.
'Fragrant Spring'.

PLATE 55.
Illustration showing the leaves and a bud of 'Fragrant Spring'.

PLATE 56.
Close-up of 'Freda'.

'Freda'

Probably the best montana for a small garden as it restricts its growth to an area of about 3m. x 3m. (10ft. x 10ft.) giving intense colour. The flower starts off with a deep mauve-red colour which fades in the centre to a pinky-mauve giving a flower of two colours. Foliage is an attractive deep bronze. Strongly recommended.

Name:	After the raiser.
Origin:	Found by Mrs Freda Deacon in her garden at Woodbridge, Suffolk, U.K. Probably a seedling from 'Pink Perfection'. Introduced by Jim Fisk in 1985.
Habit:	A compact deciduous climber up to 3m. (10ft.). Profuse flowerer. Early flowering.
Flowers:	Four tepals making single open flower; at first flower is deep mauve-red or cerise; centre of flower fades as it matures to pink-mauve; tepals – broad elliptic; conspicuous stamens; yellow anther; white filaments; pistil – silky-green fading to yellow; my own plants have produced a conspicuous sweet scent in mature flower.
Foliage:	Ternate; incised; large; bronze with red in outer part of leaflet; front of stem is red.
Special Features:	Ideal for small garden. Distinctive features are two toned pinky-red flower and bronze foliage; only 'Warwickshire Rose' has deeper colouring in leaf and flower. A.G.M. 1993.

PLATE 57.
'Freda'.

Fifty Years of Service

As the last millennium came to an end, the celebrated nursery of Jim Fisk at
Wesleton, Suffolk, U.K. closed. This after 50 years. After the disastrous
impact of stem rot (clematis wilt) at the end of the nineteenth century,
clematis production came almost to a halt. It was Jim Fisk who restored the
interest in clematis after he came home from the Royal Navy at the end of
the Second World War. He did this by careful selection of plants for
introduction. Every plant had to be distinctive and different from anything
else on the market. He hunted the world for suitable plants while staging
spectacular exhibits at the Chelsea Show. Interest in clematis returned.
Amongst his many introductions were 'Alexander', 'Freda', 'Mayleen',
'Marjorie', and 'Picton's Variety' from the Montana Group. In his last year
the superlative 'Wesselton', from the Macropetala Group, was introduced – a
last demonstration of quality.

PLATE 58.
Leaf form of 'Freda'.

PLATE 59.
The flower of 'Gothenburg'.

'Gothenburg'

This is another montana blessed with unusual foliage. On the leaflets of the dark green foliage is to be seen a central silver strip while the stem of the leaf can be red. The flower is large on long stalks. A good plant.

Name:	After town where it was raised.
Origin:	Gothenburg Botanic Gardens, Sweden, and introduced by Magnus Johnson. Known since 1995.
Habit:	A deciduous climber up to 5m. (16ft.). Moderate vigour.
Flower:	Four broad-obovate (reverse egg-shaped) tepals; flower up to 9cm. (3½in.) across; no overlap of tepals; colour is pale pink with a broad central band of violet-pink which is stronger near the base of tepal; may have a central strong purple bar on back of tepal; anthers – yellow; pistil – green fading to yellow; very long firm stems; mature flower has slight fragrance like pinks or carnations.
Foliage:	Ternate. Each leaflet is dark green or greeny-purple with central silver stripe; silver stripe is not always visible or conspicuous; sometimes stems are red.
Special Features:	Distinctive feature is the unique central silver stripe on leaflets.

PLATE 60.
The blooms of 'Gothenburg'.

Shipping Plants Home

Bearing in mind the long hazardous trip home to be endured by plants, it might be thought that seeds would be sent instead. But this was not the case. Plants were usually sent. The long journey from China via the Cape of Good Hope could take six months to Europe. They were packed into boxes. The drill was to keep the boxes on the poop of the ship away from the sea water. On fine days the box might be opened and the plants watered. At St Helena they were brought ashore and rested. Sometimes gardeners accompanied them and these were trained in the upkeep of the plants. In time they discovered the value of putting the plants in their pots some weeks before the journey. It was estimated that for every 100 plants that travelled only one survived!

PLATE 61.
Leaf form of 'Gothenburg'.

PLATE 62.
Seed head of 'Gothenburg'.

Clematis gracilifolia

This clematis from the wild, related to the montanas, is a fine garden plant. It flowers earlier than the montanas and thus extends the season of flowering of the group. Its foliage is distinctive, having small finely lobed leaflets. Its tidy habit of growth is an attraction. It is covered with round pearly-white flowers. Ideal for a small garden. A plant of charm.

Name:	'Slender leaves'.
Origin:	First found by the great Russian collector, G. N. Potanin on 28 May 1885, on his third exploration, at 9,350ft. near the Monastery, Djoni Mombo, near Siku, Western China. Found E. H. Wilson in June 1908 and again in September 1910, in West Sichuan, China, and introduced by him in 1910. Subsequently found by a number of collectors – William Purdom from Kansu, China, in 1911; George Forrest from Yunnan, China; Dr Harry Smith of Sweden from Sichuan, China, in 1935; by Christopher Grey-Wilson; by Roy Lancaster and Raymond Evison from Kangding, China, in 1981; plants from the seeds of the last expedition flowered at Treasures of Tenbury in 1984.
Habit:	Deciduous climber and scrambler. Vigorous to 3.5m. (12ft.). Profuse flowerer.
Flower:	Four obovate (reverse egg-shaped) tepals making an open cross-like flower; white; 4cm. (1½in.) across; single or clusters of 2–4 from leaf joints; anthers – pale yellow; filaments – white; pistil – green and prominent; very long stalks. My plant has no fragrance.
Foliage:	Differs from montanas in having mixed pinnate or ternate leaves; 3–7 coarse-toothed leaflets; greyish-green colour; down on stems.
Special Features:	Distinctive features are fine foliage and early flowering with small white flowers.

PLATE 64.
Clematis gracilifolia makes a striking display.

Revolutionary and Collector

Grigori Nicolaevich Potanin (1835–1920) collected *Clematis gracilifolia*. As a young man Potanin was leader of a revolutionary movement in Siberia, was jailed in 1866, but freed in 1874 due to the intercession of the leaders of the Geographical Society who he had impressed. Subsequent to his release, he agreed to lead collecting expeditions sponsored by that society. He undertook four journeys on all of which he was accompanied by Mrs Potanin. The first two were to Mongolia. The last two were to China and on the first of these he collected *C. gracilifolia*. On the last journey Mrs Potanin became very ill and died. His massive collections went to the Imperial Botanical Garden at St Petersburgh.

PLATE 65.
Clematis gracilifolia- leaf form.

PLATE 66.
Clematis gracilifolia- seed head.

'Grandiflora'

This is one of the glories of this group. It has a large white flower and makes an immense plant. It is one of the most hardy of the montanas. It is easy to grow. Highly recommended as an outstanding plant.

PLATE 67.
The striking flower of 'Grandiflora'.

Name:	Refers to its large flower.
Origin:	Collected by one of Nathaniel Wallich's collectors at Mount Pundua, Sillet Province, India in June 1829. Then called *Clematis punduana,* No. 4682 in the Wallich Collection, Kew Herbarium, U.K. Wallich gave it to the firm of Veitch of Exeter. Both it and 'Montana' flowered in their nursery in 1844 (*Hortus Veitchii* 1906). The plant is attributed to Wallich by *Hortus Veitchii*. The plant description is in the *Botanical Magazine* (t.4061) (1844) under the heading of *Montana Grandiflora'*. Also collected by E. H. Wilson at Huent Omei, China, June 1904 and Western Szechuan, China, in July 1908. Re-introduced by C. D. Brickell and A. Leslie recently from China with very large flowers; not yet available commercially.
Habit:	Deciduous climber. Very vigorous. Up to 9m. (30ft.) and beyond. Profuse flowerer. Most hardy of the montanas.
Flower:	Four, sometimes five, broad obovate tepals that do not overlap; creamy bud; white flower; yellow anthers; greeny-white filaments; pistil – green and prominent; grouped in clusters of 4-6. My plant has flowers with slight but definite scent. Flower up to 8cm. (3¼in.) across. Roy Lancaster (*Travels in China*, 1989) noted plants with flowers up to 12cm. (4½in.) across at Huadianba, China. May have tinge of red on back of tepals.
Foliage:	Large. Ternate. Mid-green. Reddy-brown stem. Hairs on stalks of leaflet.
Special Features:	Confused with *C. chrysocoma* var. *sericea* (syn: *C. spooneri*). A.G.M. 1993. Distinctive features are large white flowers borne in profusion on a large plant.

PLATE 68.
An impressive display of *clematis montana* 'Grandiflora'.

PLATE 69.
The leaf shape of 'Grandiflora'.

A celebrated Curator

Nathaniel Wallich (1786–1854) who found *C. montana* 'Grandiflora' was instrumental in building up the Calcutta Botanic Garden. He was initially the Medical Officer in the Danish settlement near Calcutta until he and the settlement were taken over by the East India Company. In due course he became Curator of the Calcutta Botanic Garden. Thereafter he was British in every sense of the word – becoming a Fellow of the Linnean Society and of the Royal Society. His massive collections at first went to the Linnean Society but were later transferred to the herbarium at Kew. His *Plantae Asiaticae Rariores* contained a fine engraving of *Clematis montana*, which he collected in Nepal in 1821, after his friend Buchanan had collected it in Nepal in 1802.

PLATE 70.
Close-up of 'Hidcote'.

'Hidcote' (syn. *C.* x *vedrariensis* 'Hidcote')

This plant, of the *vedrariensis* sub-group, has the virtue of flowering later than the montanas. The flowers are very fragrant and the flower is large. The tepals can twist attractively. The foliage is downy. It is less hardy than the montanas. Has been called a late large flowering 'Elizabeth'.

Name:	After place of origin – Hidcote Manor, Chipping Campden, Gloucestershire, U.K.
Origin:	Raised by Lawrence Johnson (1871–1958) founder of notable garden at Hidcote Manor. Probably a seedling from *C.* x *vedrariensis*. Introduced by Treasures of Tenbury, U.K., in 1968.
Habit:	Deciduous climber. Strong. To 6m. (20ft.). Profuse flowerer. Not as hardy as montanas. Need sunny sheltered aspect to prevent damage by frost.
Flower:	Single open flower; the tepals can reflex and twist; up to 11cm. (3in.); tepals – four obovate; no overlap of tepals; tepals can reflex; pale mauve-pink and strong pink around edges in young flower; fades to white with slight pink edge; white behind; anthers – yellow and green in young stamens; filament – white; connective – green in young stamens; carpels – green fading to yellow; pistil not prominent; long stalk; fragrant – strong; sweet, vanilla or magnolia.
Foliage:	Ternate, cut edges, mid-green. Large short hairs on stalk and edges and underside of leaf; top leaflet is largest; pointed leaflets.
Special Features:	Compare with 'Highdown' and 'Rosea', neither has scent.

Hidcote Manor Garden

'Hidcote' was raised at this celebrated English garden at Hidcote Bartrim, Chipping Campden, Gloucestershire, U.K. A wonderful visit for clematarians can include a visit to the memorial garden to E. H. Wilson in nearby Chipping Campden where he was born. The ten-acre Hidcote Manor Garden is on a hill top with a fine view over the Vale of Evesham. It includes a wide range of plants and trees. The garden was developed by Lawrence Johnson (1871–1958). He was also responsible for a fine garden at Menton, France.

PLATE 71.
'Hidcote'.

PLATE 72.
Leaves of 'Hidcote'.

PLATE 73.
Seed head of 'Hidcote'.

PLATE 74.
'Highdown', the most popular of the vedrariensis sub-group.

'Highdown' (syn. *C.* x *vedrariensis* 'Highdown')

'Highdown' is another vedrariensis that flowers after the montanas. The pinky-violet flower is square and slightly concave. It is moderately vigorous in a sheltered position. With 'Rosea' it is the most popular of the vedrariensis sub-group.

Name:	After property of raiser.
Origin:	Raised by Sir Fredrick Claude Stern (1884–1967) of Highdown, Goring-on-Sea, Sussex, U.K. in his remarkable chalk garden. Probably a seedling of *C.* x *vedrariensis*. Introduced by Jim Fisk in 1960.
Habit:	Deciduous climber up to 6m. (20ft.). Moderate vigour. Needs shelter.
Flower:	Four broad obovate tepals making a square concave flower; up to 8cm. (3¼in.) across; mauve-pink, colour more prominent at edges; anthers – yellow; filaments – white; carpels – yellow and not prominent; long stalks; no fragrance.
Foliage:	Small; ternate; mid-green and bronzy; hair on edge of leaflets and back of leaves; dark red colour of leaf stems.
Special Features:	Compare with 'Hidcote'. 'Highdown' has a smaller flower, a concave shape to flower to flower and leaves are smaller, more dissected and have more red on leaf stalk. Compare with 'Rosea'. 'Rosea' has much more colour and a very bronzy foliage.

A Chalk Garden

Sir Frederick Stern's (1884–1967) garden at Highdown, Goring-on-Sea, Sussex, U.K. was so chalky that he wrote a book about it (*The Chalk Garden*. 1960). The garden was on the South Downs overlooking the sea. As his interest in gardening grew he found that he was forced to grow plants that would adjust to chalk. The pH of this soil was massively alkaline. The soil had one great asset – it stored water. So great was the water retention that he could take a handful of chalk in the hottest weather and squeeze water out of it. Nevertheless, he could not persuade the Large Flowered clematis

PLATE 75.
'Highdown'.

to grow in it. So he turned his attention to the Small Flowered. He planted *C.* x *vedrariensis* and the clematis that took the name of the garden was probably a seedling from it. So big was his plant that it covered all the windows on that side of his house. The garden has been donated to the town of Worthing and is open to the public.

PLATE 76.
Leaf form of 'Highdown'.

'Jacqui'

This clematis brings an unusual virtue to the montana world – it has double, semi-double and single flowers on the same plant. The flowers are white tinged with mauve-pink. In addition it is scented. Some feel that the flowers lack colour until mature. But it may still be the best of the small white doubles. Suitable for a small garden.

Name:	After the raiser.
Origin:	Chance seedling in the garden of Jacqui Williams of Hertfordshire, U.K., an employee of Priorswood Clematis Nursery in the mid 1990s. Introduced by Pennell's Nursery, Lincoln and Priorswood Clematis Nursery, Ware, Hertfordshire, U.K. in 1998.
Habit:	Deciduous climber. Moderate vigour. Climbs to 5m. (16ft.). Good floriferous effect.
Flower:	Has single, semi-double and double forms; flowers rather green and unattractive at first; rounded flower with a circle of four tepals and up to eight staminodes like hub of a wheel; up to 7cm. (2½in.) across; tepals and staminodes are white tinged with mauve-pink; tepals and staminodes twist, fold and recurve attractively; has stamens; yellow anthers; white filaments; yellow pistil; long flower stalks; delicate fragrance.
Foliage:	Small ternate leaves. Light green.
Special Features:	Compare with other white double montanas – 'Margaret Jones', 'Pleniflora', 'Jenny Keay'. Distinctive feature is that of having single, semi-double and double flowers on the same plant. Certificate of Merit, British Clematis Society, 2002.

PLATE 78.
The blooms of 'Jacqui' make a stunning display.

PLATE 79.
An eye-catching display of the blooms of 'Jacqui'.

A Great Collector

Dr Augustine Henry (1857–1930) was the first to find a number of clematis, including *C. rubens* and *C. wilsonii*. This distinguished collector had at least two advantages over other collectors – he worked for the Chinese and could speak their language. Furthermore, he hired Chinese to collect for him. He started collecting in 1885, and soon after found *C. montana rubens*. He continued collecting until he left China in 1900. E. H. Wilson visited him on his first trip to China. Many of his collections, 150,000 specimens, went to Kew. Following his return to Britain he devoted himself to forestry.

PLATE 80.
'Lilacina' with its tinge of lilac making it different from other blooms.

'Lilacina'

This French introduction of long ago is a desirable strong growing montana. The flower has a tinge of lilac that makes it a little different from the other pink montanas. The flower is large on a long stem making it suitable for cutting. The plant is covered with bloom.

Name:	'Lilac'.
Origin:	A cross of 'Grandiflora' and 'Rubens'. Raised and introduced by Lemoine et Fils, of Nancy, France in 1910. (*The Garden* 1910, 74. 119; *Rev.Hort.* 1911, 244.)
Habit:	Deciduous climber up to 9m. (30ft.). Very flowery.
Flower:	Four tepals making cruciform flower 7½cm. (3in.) across; flowers on long stems; white background of tepal streaked with lilac-pink; anther – yellow; filament – white; pistil – green and prominent; faint fragrance.
Foliage:	Ternate. Mid-green.
Special Features:	Other montanas introduced by Lemoine at about the same time, 'Perfecta' and 'Undulata' are lost. Distinctive feature is a touch of lilac in the flower.

A Creative Act

Almost an absolute sign of a British presence anywhere in the world is the foundation of a botanic garden. This was so in India. An original act requires an original mind. So it happened in Calcutta. The Chief Judge, Sir

PLATE 81.
'Lilacina' blooms.

PLATE 82.
A profusion of 'Lilacina' blooms.

William Jones (known as 'Persian Jones' for his fluency in the Persian language) appointed to India, was exceptionally creative. He busied himself founding an Asian society, then a museum and then a botanic garden under Colonel Kyd. Soon came a sequence of exceptional superintendents – Roxburgh, Buchanan (a short time), and the brilliant Dane, Wallich. It was to Roxburgh in Calcutta that Buchanan sent his collected material. It was Roxburgh who supplied him with botanical staff. The Calcutta Botanic Garden remains as one of the foremost botanic gardens of the world.

PLATE 83.
The attractive blooms of 'Margaret Jones'.

'Margaret Jones'

A double white flower. This plant adds charm. Needs sunny position. Merits of small size of plant and double flowers is countered by some who claim lack of impact in the bloom. Supporters point to the irregular early flower that can intrigue as it looks like a bird taking off. It has a plant quality that will attract some. Suitable for a small garden.

Name:	After mother of finder.
Origin:	Chance seedling from 'Rubens' in garden of Mrs Ann Smyth, Hoveton, Norfolk. Introduced by Ruth Gooch of Thorncroft Clematis Nursery, Norfolk, U.K., in 1991.
Habit:	Deciduous climber or semi-shrub. Moderate vigour. Can be floriferous. Climbs up to 3m. (10ft.). Needs sunny aspect.
Flower:	Rounded flower; four thin outer tepals and shorter inner pistiloides; tepals and pistiloides may stand outwards and give an attractive uneven appearance; up to 5cm. (2in.) across; colour – creamy with tinge of green; prominent green pistil; long flower stalk; no fragrance. Flowers late in main group.
Foliage:	Small mid-green ternate leaves.
Special Features:	Compare with other white doubles – 'Jacqui' and 'Pleniflora'.

PLATE 84.
'Margaret Jones' blooms in abundance.

Chance Seedlings

Your montanas, and most of your clematis, set seed every year. The seeds are supplied with a feathery tail which makes it ideal for floating away in the breeze. Some will float into your own garden. They may find a receptive soil and grow into seedlings. Surprisingly, they may do best in your gritty paths rather than the beds. You can 'pot up' these seedlings, if you have the time. Next year it may be large enough to produce a bloom. That is usually the moment of disappointment. They are usually inferior to their parent plant. Chances of success? – perhaps 1–100. If you feel the plant is different, apply the acid test: 'is it distinctively different from any known plant in its group?' If it is get an expert opinion from an experienced gardener or nursery. Even then you must apply a further test – after three years in the garden, can you say it is garden worthy – free of disease, vigorous, hardy and floriferous? Too few clematis today go through this last stage and are hurriedly put on the market – to the disappointment of the purchaser who may turn his back on clematis.

PLATE 85.
A single, delicate bloom of 'Margaret Jones'.

PLATE 86.
The vigorous double blooms of 'Marjorie'.

'Marjorie'

This is one of the more vigorous double montanas. The colour is interesting; against a background of cream-yellow there is a salmon pink suffusion. For the montanas this has a long flowering period. It is a montana that arouses strong passions; either enthusiastic support or damning derision. When it does well it can be breathtaking.

Name:	After the raiser.
Origin:	Seedling of 'White Fragrance' in the garden of Miss Marjorie Free of Westleton, Suffolk, U.K. Introduced by Jim Fisk of Westleton in 1980.
Habit:	Deciduous climber. Very vigorous and can climb up to 9m. (30ft.). Profuse flowerer.
Flower:	Double; four tepals are creamy-yellow with a suffusion of salmon pink; there may be two circles of inner pistillodes; these are narrower and shorter than the tepals with a stronger colour than tepals; pistil is prominent and cream; flowers on long stems; slight fragrance.
Foliage:	Ternate. Mid-green with brown stems.
Special Features:	Long flowering period. Flowers later than the average montana. Compare with 'Broughton Star'.

PLATE 87.
'Marjorie' and a riot of bloom.

A Statue for Robert Fortune?

While we know Robert Fortune (1822–1880) for his prodigous plant collecting and in particular for bringing *Clematis lanuginosa* from China to England and so transforming the hybridising of clematis, probably his major achievement was to bring tea plants and tea seeds from China to India. He collected from the best tea areas in China. The plants were then packed into Wardian Cases. As tea seeds are only viable for a short time, he also planted tea seeds in seed boxes. These germinated on the voyage and tea seedlings were available on arrival. He introduced 100,000 plants and seedlings to India, transforming the economy of that country. His admirers think he did more for India than the generals, politicians and economists. They still await a statue for him!

PLATE 88.
A single flower of 'Marjorie'.

PLATE 89.
The beautiful blooms of 'Mayleen'.

'Mayleen'

This plant has everything you expect of a montana – immense growth, gorgeous scent, lovely flower, ease of growth. Many years ago Jim Fisk said to me, 'This is the montana to grow.' The years have confirmed his choice. Outstanding.

Name:	Customer at Chelsea Flower Show brought in a cutting of a montana to Jim Fisk that had been raised by her friend Mayleen. He named it after Mayleen.
Origin:	Introduced by Jim Fisk in 1984.
Habit:	Deciduous climber. Up to 10m. (33ft.) in height and spread. Very vigorous. Very profuse flowerer.
Flower:	Four broad obovate (reverse egg-shaped) tepals; flower has a ruffled surface; makes a square flower and tepals touch and overlap; deep violet pink colour that fades with time; stronger colour in centre of flower; flower up to 8cm. (3¼in.) across; anther – yellow; filament – white; pistil – green and prominent; in clusters up to six in number; strong fragrance.
Foliage:	Ternate. Mid-green or bronze or semi-bronze.
Special Features:	Compare with 'Vera' which has a gappy flower with no overlap of tepals. AGM 2002.

PLATE 90.
'Mayleen'- a single beautiful bloom.

The Tallest Montana

People trade experiences about this. The tallest accounts are usually about the giants like 'Mayleen', 'Grandiflora', *montana*, 'Elizabeth', 'Pink Perfection' and 'Rubens'. But not always. By a chance combination of excellent climate, position, soil and nutriment one of the usually less tall montanas will take off. This makes it difficult sometimes to give the optimum size of a given montana. Someone comes along with – 'mine is twice, or five times, that', or – 'mine is only half that'. I have seen montanas up very high trees. One I remember seemed to have got 12m. (40ft.) up an enormous tree, colonised all around it, and then a strand had gone on another 12m. (40ft.) to the very top of this tree and colonised there. How they climb is fascinating. They throw out a strand in the wind and sooner or later this comes up against a branch and fixes itself to it. The rest cling to and climb up this fixed strand.

PLATE 91.
'Mayleen'- seed head.

PLATE 92.
The deep pink flowers of 'New Dawn'.

'New Dawn'

This plant has one of the deepest pink flowers in the group. Selected in The Netherlands, it was expected to replace 'Tetrarose'. It has not done that but both plants are very desirable. If choosing between them then probably 'Tetrarose' scores by having a larger flower. 'New Dawn' is suitable for a small garden.

Name:	To emphasise its newness.
Origin:	Selected by the Experimental Station, Boskoop, The Netherlands, 1992.
Habit:	Deciduous climber. Moderately vigorous to 4.5m. (15ft.).
Flower:	Four broad obovate tepals which may partly overlap and recurve; deep pinky-mauve colour; up to 6.5cm. (2½in.) across; anther – yellow; filament – white; pistil – green; long flower stems; usually said not to be fragrant, I could detect slight scent in a mature flower.
Foliage:	Ternate; mid-green; a little bronze in young leaves.
Special Features:	Compare with 'Tetrarose' which has finer cut, more bronze foliage, and larger flower with strong fragrance.

The Dreaded Clematis Wilt

Happily, very happily, clematis wilt does not affect the montanas. Recent research has also shown that it only affects one out of twelve groups of clematis – the Early Large Flowered. Interestingly, we now know that the

PLATE 93.
'New Dawn'- flower and bud.

wilt first attacks the leaves. It then spreads along the stalk of the leaf to the node of the stem and gets into the stem there. This causes rotting of the stem – 'stem rot'. In New Zealand they showed that when the fungus reached the nodes of the montanas, the plant rejects the fungus, will not let it in and, if hard driven, it will seal the stem and make the leaf drop off. This capacity is a big plus for the montanas. If your montana droops, flops, or wilts, it will not be due to 'stem rot' (clematis wilt) but some other cause of drooping, flopping or wilting – of which there are a number.

PLATE 94.
'New Dawn'.

PLATE 95.
'New Dawn'- seed head.

PLATE 96.
The pale pink flowers of 'Odorata'.

'Odorata'

This is a strongly growing floriferous montana with a pale pink flower and, as the name suggests, a strong scent. It is reminiscent of 'Elizabeth' but has a smaller flower and rather less colour in the bloom.

Name:	Indicates fragrance of plant. (Countess Sarah Amehurst who found a *Clematis montana* in 1827 near Simla, North India, referred to *C. montana* as 'Odorata', a name now obsolete).
Origin:	Introduced in 1982 by Jim Fisk who states in his catalogue (1986) 'an old variety re-introduced'. Magnus Johnson describes a *montana* 'Odorata Trelleborg' found by his son, Göran Johnson, in South Sweden in 1970. Fisk's plant is generally available and described here.
Habit:	Deciduous climber. Very vigorous up to 9m. (30ft.). Very floriferous.
Flower:	Four elliptic tepals that may recurve and do not overlap; colour is that of flecks of pink on white; yellow anther; white filament; green prominent pistil; strong perfume reminiscent of hyacinth or vanilla; flowers early.
Foliage:	Ternate, tidy, mid-green, bronze young leaves.
Special Features:	Heavily scented. Compare with others in the pale pink flower group.

PLATE 97.
'Odorata' produces a mass of sweet-scented blooms.

Do You Want Scent?

Most people do want scent in their montanas. One noble customer of Jim Fisk thought he did too. He wanted a scented clematis under his window. Jim planted an 'Elizabeth' for him – it gives gorgeous sweet scent of course. In a couple of years the client called. 'That thing you planted for me, Jim. Take it out. It stinks.' Most people do like scent but to try and describe it is difficult. There is no accepted classification so one compares with another flower, or plant, or fruit, or animal scent or a product like chocolate. 'White Fragrance' is indeed very fragrant. I used it for experimentation with a group of people. Each was seen alone; once a name is given the rest of the group smell that. They were asked to describe the scent of 'White Fragrance'. Answers: 'narcissus', 'privet', 'lemon', 'daisies', 'vanilla', 'French pâtisserie', 'bluebells', 'musty', 'sweet', 'carnation', 'honey' and 'hot chocolate'. The last is interesting. Christopher Lloyd described it as such. My wife did also. They have one thing in common – both are superb cooks. So they have the smells of the kitchen as well as the garden to draw upon.

PLATE 98.
'Odorata' seed head.

PLATE 99.
A single scented flower of 'Olga'.

'Olga'

This splendid strong plant has scented pink flowers and a long flowering period. This is a plant of distinct foliage; the foliage is suffused with purple, both in the front and the back of the leaves. The leaves are most attractive as they move in the breeze. It all makes for a splendid plant, attractive for its leaves alone.

Name:	Unknown.
Origin:	Unknown.
Habit:	Deciduous climber. Very vigorous. Climbs up to 6m. (20ft.).
Flower:	Four broad obovate (reverse egg-shaped) tepals that make a flat open flower and overlap at base; clear mauve-pink colour; up to 6.5cm. (2½in.) across; long firm stalks; anther – yellow; filament – white; pistil – green and prominent; strongly scented; long flowering period.
Foliage:	Ternate; front of leaves suffused with purple; especially at edge; back of leaves are shiny purple and catch the eye.
Special Features:	Attractive for its foliage which is its distinctive feature and a very tidy and round flower shape.

Mulching

We all have our favourite mulching material. In my experience the best natural product is leaf mould. It is nature's own. It not only prevents vaporisation but also feeds. It is not, however, always easy to obtain. Lawn

PLATE 100.
The blooms of 'Olga' make a colourful display.

mowings, stones, grit, bark, moss or peat may have to be substituted depending upon what is available at the time. I have, over many years, come to value one product – capillary matting. Washington in the USA has an extreme climate. Situated on the Potomac River, it is tropical in summer and icy in winter. There all the trees and shrubs have ground cover of capillary matting and over it a pile of insulating material like bark. Water gets through and you can lift it aside to apply fertiliser. The UK Forestry Commision, after research, recommended matting as the best method. I am inclined to agree. Combined with the 'leaky pipe' method of watering they make ideal companions. Do not, however, overwater as that kills more plants than underwatering.

PLATE 101.
'Olga'– leaf form.

PLATE 102.
'Picton's Variety'.

'Picton's Variety'

This plant is justly popular for a height that makes it suitable for small gardens. In addition the flower is an attractive deep pink. The foliage appeals for its bronzeness. A bonus is the spicy fragrance. It is not, however, easy to grow.

Name:	After its raiser.
Origin:	Percy Picton had seeds from a *C. montana rubens* growing at Gravetye Manor; a seedling became 'Picton's Variety' in the mid '50s. Introduced by Jim Fisk in 1956.
Habit:	Deciduous climber. Makes short plant up to 4.5m. (15ft.). Not as easy to grow as some. Has been said to be liable to wilt but this will not be caused by 'stem rot' (phoma clemitidina) but other hazards that cause wilting. Tender. Protect in hard winters.
Flower:	Four tepals that may recurve; many have five or six tepals; up to 8.5cm. (3¼in.) across; deep mauve-pink throughout; anther – creamy-yellow; pistil – green; filament – white; fair spicy fragrance.
Foliage:	Ternate. Light bronze. This is lighter than expected for a deep coloured flower.
Special Features:	Compare with 'Veitch' which has smaller flower.

PLATE 103.
An attractive floral grouping of 'Picton's Variety'.

A Fine Gardener

Percy Picton, who raised 'Picton's Variety', had the finest possible tuition. He was a gardener at Gravetye Manor, the home of the redoubtable pioneering William Robinson. In addition he worked with Ernest Markham, who was Robinson's head gardener and friend. Robinson was enfeebled in his old age, and one of Percy's tasks was to push Robinson around the garden. Many would have paid big money to do that! After Robinson died he was gardener at Hagley Court and introduced the excellent 'Hagley Hybrid'. It is possible that he brought a seedling with him from Gravetye Manor and that this was one of the many seedlings the great French hybridiser, Morel, gave to Robinson when, fed up with stem rot (clematis wilt), he gave up his nursery in favour of landscape gardening. Percy Picton never hybridised but knew a good clematis when he saw it – and introduced it, usually through Jim Fisk.

PLATE 104.
'Picton's Variety'- single flower.

91

PLATE 105.
The splendid blooms of 'Pink Perfection'.

'Pink Perfection'

Tales abound of the mighty plants produced by this montana. Not only is the plant large but covered in bloom. The perfume is considerable but not as overwhelming as in its rival 'Elizabeth'.

Name:	Descriptive.
Origin:	A seedling of a *C. montana rubens* raised by George Jackman & Son, Woking, U.K. Rowland Jackman mentions it in *Planter's Handbook*, 1952–53, and introduced it at that time.
Habit:	Deciduous climber. Very vigorous – up to 9m. (30ft.) and beyond. Floriferous.
Flower:	Four broad tepals which may overlap and tips may recurve; up to 7cm. (2⅓in.) across; colour is white suffused with pale mauve-pink which is stronger at centre (reverse of 'Elizabeth'); anther – yellow; filament – white; connective – green; pistil – dark green and prominent; distinct sweet perfume (but less than 'Elizabeth').
Foliage:	Ternate. Mid-green. Marbled.
Special Features:	Compare with 'Elizabeth' which has more perfume and slightly more colour.
	Colour is stronger at edges in 'Elizabeth' but suffused throughout tepal in 'Pink Perfection' or at the centre of the tepal. It also has broader overlapping tepals than 'Elizabeth'.

PLATE 106.
An attractive array of blooms of 'Pink Perfection'.

PLATE 107.
A single flower- 'Pink Perfection'.

PLATE 108.
'Pink Perfection- seed head.

A Hazardous Life

The life of Dr Clarke Abel (1780–1826) illustrates the hazards of seeking a livelihood in the Far East. He was appointed naturalist to accompany the Ambassador to China, Lord Ameherst, in 1816 on his visit to the Chinese Emperor in Peking. After a long journey the visit was a failure and the discomforted Ambassador started his return journey that very day. They transversed China from Peking to Canton and Dr Abel assiduously collected plants every inch of the way. Then with his magnificent collection he boarded the warship 'Alceste' in Canton, but the ship hit a reef in the Caspan Straits. All personnel were saved but the collection of plants was lost. Three hundred packets of seeds had been saved but a naval officer lacked room for his spare clothes in the boat and so the seeds were dumped! Medical men are not immune from the plagues of those times. When accompanying Lord Amehurst, now Governor-General of India on a journey through the Northern Provinces of India, he was stricken down and died at Cawnpore in 1826. Had he survived he would later have no doubt accompanied Countess Amehurst on her finding of *C. montana* at Simla. The genus *Abelia* is named after him.

PLATE 109.
The double white flowers of 'Pleniflora'.

'Pleniflora'

This is an introduction, a double white, from Switzerland that competes with the doubles from the U.K. and New Zealand. This one scores for its attractive bell-shaped buds and its profusion of flowers. It comes late in the montana season and so helps to extend that season. The initial flowers may be single followed by double flowers later.

Name:	'Double flower'.
Origin:	A seedling from *C. montana* raised and introduced by Hans Reudi Horn-Gfeller at Merligen, Switzerland, before 1980.
Habit:	Deciduous climber. Moderate vigour to 3.5m. (12ft.). A profusion of flowers. Not very hardy. At one time there may be single, semi-double or double flowers.
Flower:	Four outer obovate tepals; inner group of pistillodes; sometimes making single or semi-double or double flower; bud is an attractive bell shape and greeny-white in colour often pointing upwards; tepals and pistillodes are greeny-white fading to white, often green at tip of tepal; pistiloides may be tinged pink at back, tip and edges; flower up to 5cm. (2in.) across; prominent greeny-white pistil; no fragrance; late flush of flowers will be double.
Foliage:	Ternate. Light green.
Special Features:	Compare with other double white montanas – 'Jacqui', 'Margaret Jones', 'Jenny Keay'.

PLATE 110.
Blooms of 'Pleniflora'.

PLATE 111.
Seed head of 'Pleniflora'.

The Wardian Case

The shipping of plants home was transformed by the invention of a new tool by Dr Nathaniel Ward described in a book in 1842. His case was like a small portable greenhouse. It worked on the same principle as putting a plastic bag over a pot today; any water evaporating from the soil collects on the plastic and creates humidity. The process is self-perpetuating and fresh water is not required. Plants, some 10–14 days before travel are planted in 9in. of soil in the case. Moss placed on the surface of the soil reduces evaporation. The plants now have water and light through the glass. No salt water can enter. Robert Fortune used Wardian Cases on a big scale. On his first expedition, of 250 plants sent to London, 215 survived. It was a revolution in plant care.

PLATE 112.
The attractive coloured bloom of 'Rosea'.

'Rosea' (syn. *C.* x *vedrariensis* 'Rosea')

This plant, as a true vedrariensis, flowers later than the montanas. It needs a sheltered position. The flowers retain their colour well. Lovely bronze foliage – especially in young plant. Has been termed 'a pink chrysocoma'. A wonderful plant in a sympathetic climate.

Name:	After 'rosy', the colour of the flower. Today's flower is paler than 'rose'.
Origin:	Messrs. Vilmorin, having produced *C.* x *vedrariensis* by a cross of *C. montana rubens* and *C. chrysocoma*, decided to make further crosses in 1917. They crossed *C. chrysocoma* var *sericea* (syn. *C. spooneri*) with *C.* x *vedrariensis* and *C. montana* 'Rubens'. The results looked alike and both were given the name *C. spooneri* 'Rosea', this is now called 'Rosea'. (To add to the confusion the term *C. spooneri* 'Rosea' is used for *C. vedrariensis* and 'Highdown' and 'Rosea'.)
Habit:	Deciduous climber. Climbs up to 3.5m. (12ft.). Not hardy. Needs shelter.
Flower:	Four obovate tepals; cup shaped at first and then makes open flat flower; up to 6cm. (2¼in.) across; light rosy-mauve throughout flower but more pronounced in centre of flower; keeps colour well; anther – yellow; filament – white; carpels – greeny-yellow; long hairy stalks; no fragrance.
Foliage:	Ternate; large; heavy reddy-bronzing of young leaves; stalk is dark browny-red in front; hairs on leaflets, leaf stalks, back of tepals, flower stalks.
Special Features:	Note bronzing of leaves. Compare with *C. chrysocoma* and the other three from the vedrariensis sub-group.

PLATE 113.
'Rosea' makes a striking display.

Preserving Plants

Not only did collectors send plants home, unsuccessfully at first until the invention of the Wardian Case, they also collected seeds. In addition specimens of plants were dried and pressed to preserve them. The process is remarkably simple and the results can preserve most of the features of

PLATE 114.
'Rosea'– leaf form.

a plant for centuries. Most find their way to the herbaria of the large botanical gardens of the world. The whole process involves collecting, drying, pressing, mounting and labelling.

Try placing the stem, leaves and flowers of a small plant between a pile of old papers. Place some old books or old telephone directories on top for extra weight. After three days replace the papers as they have become soggy. The new dry papers will prevent the plant material getting fungi. During the process of replacing the papers, you can tidy up any folded flowers or leaves. Put some extra papers on top but not heavy weight. Leave for three weeks, open – and be amazed.

PLATE 115.
A striking flower of 'Rubens' contrasts with the bronzy foliage.

'Rubens' (syn. *C. montana* var. *rubens*)

When E. H. Wilson the great plant collector intrduced 'Rubens' from central China a hundred years ago it was a sensation. The white 'Montana' epitomised India, and the pink 'Rubens', China. It has all the attributes you need in a montana – lovely large pink flower against bronzy foliage; delicious scent and vigour. It has parented a number of montanas; few of them can challenge the parent.

Name:	'Reddish'.
Origin:	First found by Dr Augustine Henry (1857–1931) in Hupeh, China, probably after he started collecting in 1885. Described by Otto Kuntze in 1886. Re-discovered by E. H. Wilson in central China in May–June 1900. Seeds sent to Messrs. J. Veitch and Sons at their Coombe Wood Nursery, Kingston, U.K. A number of seedlings were produced from seed. This seedling, and it alone, was used for propagating stock in 1903. As it seeds easily many seedlings have been produced, many not the quality of the original. E. H. Wilson emphasised two identifying features – 'rose pink' flowers and 'very dark' foliage.
Flower:	Four broad-elliptic tepals make a compact, almost square flower; tepals may twist and fold; up to 7cm. (2⅔in.) across; pink-mauve throughout petals that fades with maturity; anthers – greeny-yellow; filament – white; pistil – silky-green and prominent; flowers in clusters up to six from leaf axils; deep fragrance – vanilla.
Foliage:	Ternate. Small. Bronzy leaves. Purple stems.
Special Features:	'Rubens' available today has less colour than described by Wilson. It is, however, still a fine plant. A.G.M. 1993. Withdrawn 2002.

PLATE 116.
Blooms of 'Rubens' light up a leafy background.

PLATE 117.
A single bloom of 'Rubens'.

PLATE 118.
'Rubens' – seed head.

Judging a Plant

Our idea of a garden-worthy plant is one with the following attributes – strong grower, withstands any climate, accepts any position, is covered with bloom, fascinating shape to the flower and scent you can smell some distance away. In practice we have to settle for less. In fact we have to choose a plant that will grow in the conditions we have – and much less than ideal. So we have to see what the plant offers and find if that suits our requirements. Plants vary in their features. One will suit one set of conditions and one another. The above thoughts are stimulated by the montana 'East Malling' It was meant to be an improved 'Rubens'. But improved in what way? Its foliage is less attractive than 'Rubens'. The flower is less attractive than 'Rubens'. The flower is smaller than 'Rubens'. It has less scent than 'Rubens'. Is it better in any way? It is – in its vigour. On that criteria alone it is improved. But on no other. So it depends what you want.

PLATE 119.
The deep pink bloom of 'Tetrarose'- the largest of all the montanas.

'Tetrarose'

This montana has been a delight in our gardens for forty years. It has glowing deep pink flowers which are the largest montana blooms when the plant does well. It is very floriferous. Not over vigorous and thus one of the best for a small garden. It has a sweet fragrance. It was thought that 'New Dawn' would replace it but in the event it has held its place in the garden.

Name:	Refers to four rose coloured tepals.
Origin:	Artificial production, making a tetrapod at Proefstation voor de Boomkwekerij, Boskoop (see also page 60), in 1960 – from 'Rubens'.
Habit:	Deciduous climber. Moderate vigour up to 6m. (20ft.). Very flowery. May need protection in frosty areas.
Flower:	Four thick broad elliptic tepals make a single open, slightly 'cupped' flower; deep pinky-purple throughout tepal; up to 10cm. (4in.) across; many prominent stamens; anthers – yellow; filament – white; green prominent pistil; fragrance in mature blooms – sweet.
Foliage:	Ternate. Large. Pointed. Bronzy and dark green. Red tinge to stems.
Special Features:	Compare with 'New Dawn'. 'Tetrarose' has larger bloom with more colour; it has more scent than 'New Dawn' and the benefit of bronze foliage. Not always easy to propagate. A.G.M. 1993.

Carolus Linnaeus

Buchanan's era came after that of the great Swedish botanist, Carolus Linnaeus (1707–1778). Linnaeus having studied in Holland became Professor of Medicine at Uppsala. Then he and the Professor of Botany changed places! This is not as peculiar as it might seem. The only drugs available to a physician were herbs. Thus a medical training involved extensive study of plants. Identifying the right plant was crucial. The search for new herbs was another compelling activity. Linnaeus tranformed nomenclature in botany with his binomal system published in his *Species Plantarum* in 1753. His country home was an idyllic spot. But life with his family was not always easy. He could be termed 'hen pecked'. No wonder he retired so often to his shack on the hill beyond the house and in the most glorious wild garden in the world. Son of a church minister he went dutifully to church – accompanied by his dog. He stayed for one hour exactly and left, even if the preacher was in mid-sentence. Sometimes he failed to get to church and the dog would go alone. The latter also left exactly after one hour!

PLATE 120.
'Tetrarose' blooms.

PLATE 121.
'Tetrarose' makes a striking display of colour.

PLATE 122.
Small blooms of 'Veitch' but with intense pink flowers.

'Veitch'

A long lost montana is just being brought back to cultivation. Another for the small garden. A smaller plant than most, it scores from the intense pink of its blooms. The flowers are set off by bronzy foliage.

Name:	After the nursery that introduced it.
Origin:	Collected in the wild in China by their own collector from the nursery of Messrs. Veitch, Coombe Wood, Kingston, Surrey, U.K. 'early this century'. Author's plant from an old specimen carefully tended by John and Sarah Philips, Roundway, Devizes, U.K.
Habit:	Deciduous climber. Moderate vigour to 3.5m. (12ft.).
Flower:	Four or five oblong tepals; if four tepals, makes a cruciform flower, if five tepals, makes a round flower; rosy coloured bud; deep pinky-purple throughout flower; retains colour well; up to 5.5cm. (2in.) across; anther – yellow; filament – white; pistil – green and prominent; some scent in mature flower.
Foliage:	Ternate; small; greeny-bronze; bronzy young leaves.
Special Features:	Compare with 'Picton's Variety'. 'Veitch' has a globular bud, four or five tepals, less bronzy leaves, and rather less colour in the mature bloom.
	'Veitch' has much more colour in the flower than 'Rubens'.

PLATE 123.
A cascade of colour from the blooms of 'Veitch'.

PLATE 124.
'Veitch'- single bloom.

PLATE 125.
'Veitch'- seed head.

An Enterprising Company

The horticultural firm of James Veitch & Sons Ltd. of Chelsea had a history over many generations from their foundation by John Veitch at Exeter in 1832. Such were their resources that they could send out plant hunters. It was one of these who found Veitch's form of montana – no doubt attracted by its very deep colour. Their most famous collector was E. H. Wilson who found *C. montana rubens* in China. Of the many seedlings grown from its seed they picked out the seedling with the deep pink colour and dark foliage. This was 'Rubens'. Until that moment montanas were known for their white colour and therefore the pink must have been a sensation. A history of the Veitch 'Rise and Progress' and a list of the most remarkable of their introductions appeared as *Hortus Veitchii* in 1906. The dynasty came to an end in 1914.

PLATE 126.
'Vera' has abundant scent and attractive pink blooms.

'Vera'

This is a fine plant for covering a large area with bloom. Lovely pink colour. Very floriferous. Abundant scent is a bonus.

Name:	Female English name.
Origin:	No specific information but believed to have been raised in Cornwall, U.K. towards the middle of the last century. Probably introduced by Treasures of Tenbury in 1984.
Habit:	Deciduous climber. Very vigorous. Height to 9m. (30ft.). Profuse flowerer. May need protection in frosty areas.
Flower:	Four obovate tepals; no overlap of tepals and flower gappy; makes large flower to 9.5cm. (3½in.); on strong stalk; violet-pink colour which is lighter in centre of tepal; prominent stamens; anther – yellow; filament – white; strong scent; up to six flowers in a cluster.
Foliage:	Ternate; large; mid-green; rough texture.
Special Features:	Compare with 'Mayleen'. 'Vera' has larger foliage with 'gappy' flower.

A Hasty Deal

When Carolus Linnaeus died in 1778 he left behind a vast collection of herbarium specimens and a considerable library. His wife and two daughters, having inherited his property, decided to sell his collections. They had in mind the sum of 1,000 guineas (a guinea = 21 English shillings).

PLATE 127.
A single bloom of 'Vera'.

PLATE 128.
'Vera'- seed head.

They targeted the wealthy Sir Joseph Banks, a great botanist and collector. But he declined to buy. There was some need for haste. The King of Sweden was travelling abroad but was soon to return. The ladies surmised that he would pressure them to send the collections to Uppsala University – and at a sum of much less than 1,000 guineas. J. E. Smith, Banks' friend, ageed to buy them and the collections were immediately sent by ship to London. The King of Sweden returned, was furious and sent a ship in pursuit. This, however, was unsuccessful and Smith now owned the collections. Upon his death, a public subscription bought the collections for the Linnean Society which Smith had founded. The Linnean Society also holds Buchanan's specimens from Nepal, including *C. montana*. They had been given by Buchanan to Smith.

PLATE 129.
'Warwickshire Rose' with its distinctive deep pink colour.

'Warwickshire Rose'

This has the deepest pink colour of all the montanas. These are set off againt the darkest foliage in all the montanas. This combination makes a showy plant perhaps best seen from a short distance; the individual blooms are small and its impact is created by the mass of bloom.

Name:	'Warwickshire' indicates the raiser's county in the U.K. 'Rose' indicates raiser's mother.
Origin:	Garden designer, John Williams, had his attention drawn to the plant by the bronzy foliage sprouting from a crack between paving stones. Probably seedling of 'Rubens'. Introduced in 1997.
Habit:	Deciduous climber. Vigorous. Climbs to 6m. (20ft.).
Flower:	Four elliptic tepals with deep cerise colour, lightest at centre and deepest at edge; occasionally has disfiguring purple spots on tepals; broad white bar on back of tepal; anther – yellow; filament – green; pistil – green and very prominent; long stalks; faint fragrance on mature flowers.
Foliage:	Ternate; fine large dark green or dark bronze, almost black; mid-green vein; light green on reverse side of leaflets.
Special Features:	Compare with 'Freda', the leaves of which are not as dark as this plant and its flowers have rounder tepals and are larger.

PLATE 130.
An attractive display of 'Warwickshire Rose'.

PLATE 131.
'Warwickshire Rose'- single bloom.

PLATE 132.
Seed head of 'Warwickshire Rose'.

Aristocrats of the Garden

The above book described what E. H. Wilson regarded as the most desirable plants for the garden. It gives scarce mention to the montanas. However, in his next volume, in 1828, *More Aristocrats of the Garden*, he is more forthcoming and includes a paragraph on the montanas with a photograph of *Clematis wilsonii*. The paragraph includes:

'There is a summer-blooming sort (var. *Wilsonii*) and another (var. *rubens*) with dark foliage. These two varieties I discovered and introduced from China some twenty-five years ago and experts acclaim them to be among the most notable additions to gardens in recent times. The variety *rubens* is hardier than the typical *C. montana*, flowers regularly every season and is readily increased by cuttings.'

PLATE 133.
A profusion of 'White Fragrance' blooms.

'White Fragrance'

This is a most desirable plant and controversy as to its origin can be ignored.
It has flourished because of its attractive, narrow, wavy tepals and its vigour.
It is also covered with flowers and there is its wonderful fragrance. It extends
the flowering period for the montanas by flowering towards the end of the
main group of montanas.

Name:	Describes the impression created by this large, very fragrant, white plant. It is a cascade of white.
Origin:	Unknown. Appeared in Jim Fisk's catalogue as far back as 1982. No association with E. H. Wilson (see Historical Notes, Chapter VII.) but often, wrongly, named *C. wilsonii*.
Habit:	Deciduous climber. Vigorous. Climbs up to 9m. (30ft.). Profuse flowerer. In my garden it flowers towards the end of the main crop, coinciding with flowering of 'Grandiflora'.
Flower:	Four long oblong tepals that often fold at the middle of the tepal; may recurve at tip and may also twist; cream at first then white in colour; mucronate (sharp tip to tepal at point) wavy edge; up to 7cm. (2½in.) across; stamens prominent; anther – yellow; filament – white; pistil – green and prominent; long stalks; very fragrant.
Foliage:	Ternate; elliptic leaflets; serrated; mid-green; stems mid-green.
Special Features:	Has no link with E. H. Wilson. However, as it flowers late, towards the end of the main crop, it may have been mistakenly associated with the true *C. wilsonii* which also flowers late, but two months later. On comparison *C. wilsonii* is seen to be a very different plant from 'White Fragrance'. (See Chapter VII Historical Notes.) It is unlikely to be the lost 'Undulata'. (See Lost Montanas on page 141.)

Naming A Plant

Not always as easy as it seems. Sometimes it is simple – name after the hybridist, the raiser, the introducer or members of their family. 'Freda' would be a case in point being named after Mrs Freda Deacon, (Freda Deacon of Woodbridge, the raiser). Naming after a client of the nursery introducing the plant was another option. No disadvantage if a plant

PLATE 134.
'White Fragrance'.

could be associated with the nobility through an aristocratic client. The place the plant was raised or introduced could be used e.g. 'Hidcote' after Hidcote Manor, 'Highdown' after Sir Fredrick Stern's home, 'Broughton Star' after Broughton, Lancashire. A feature of the plant could be introduced in the title e.g. 'Fragrant Spring' denoting time of flowering and its scent; 'Odorata' signifying its scent; 'Grandiflora' indicating a large flower; 'Pink Perfection' indicating its colour; 'Rubens' again for its colour. 'Warwickshire Rose' included its place of finding and a relative named Rose. *C. wilsonii* was named after the collector E. H. Wilson. *C. wilsonii* was given to two plants, only one of which was associated with Wilson. The other, an excellent plant, had been described by Christopher Lloyd as being 'a sheet of white', a cascade. Why not name the plant 'White Cascade'? So be it. But I discovered that there was already a clematis called 'White Cascade'. So what now? It became 'White Fragrance'!

PLATE 135.
'White Fragrance' makes an eye-catching display.

PLATE 136.
'Peveril' flowers displaying their unusually long stamens.

'Wilsonii' (syn. 'Peveril')

This is a plant worth growing for its very late flowering (late summer – early autumn) and thus two months later than the main group. It also has an unusual flower, a large white flower, with shimmering long stamens. On the negative side it is said to be difficult to propagate and to grow.

Name:	After its collector E. H. Wilson.
Origin:	First discovered by Dr Augustine Henry in Yunnan before 1888. Later, in 1904, discovered in China by E. H. Wilson when collecting for Messrs Veitch. Collected later, in 1907, 1908, 1910, when Wilson was collecting for Arnold Arboretum. Veitch distributed it as *Clematis repens*. In June 1986, Mr. Lawrence Banks (I.C.S. Newsletter Vol.3 No.1) reported that a plant of *C. wilsonii* was growing in Hergest Croft Garden, Kington, U.K., probably planted by his grandfather before the First World War. It came to be known as *C. wilsonii* Hergest Form. In 1989 Barry Fretwell in his *Clematis* reported that 'a few years ago' he was sent seed of a montana 'close to' *C. wilsonii*. It is known as 'Peveril'. Examining the Hergest Form and 'Peveril' together reveals that they are identical. (For further information see Chapter VII, Historical Notes).
Habit:	Deciduous climber. Up to 6m. (20ft.) when it does well.
Flower:	Three or usually four obovate, oblong, thick, fleshy tepals; tepals sometimes notched (retused) and usually mucronulate (pointed at tip); tepal may recurve along edges or at tip;

	uneven edge to tepal; white; many (60–70) prominent long stamens up to 2.5cm. (1in.); outside of tepals downy with yellowish hairs; 7.5cm. (3in.) across; prominent carpels – yellowish-green; anthers – yellow; filaments – white; flower on long downy stem; no scent; flowers later than any other montana – into mid- and late summer. I have seen a flower in late October; this had a slight scent.
Foliage:	Ternate; opposite; serrated; stalk of terminal leaflet three times length of lateral leaflets; downy underneath on vein; mid-green colour with dark brown stems; deeply veined leaves – sunk above, raised underneath. Bronzed edge in autumn.
Special Features:	Photos and figures of 'Peveril' in Barry Fretwell's *Clematis*. *C. wilsonii* in E. H. Wilson's *More Aristocrats of the Garden*, and *C. wilsonii* in *Bot. Magazine* (1911) agree. Note the thick, mucronated (pointed) tepals, many long stamens and veined leaves.

'Chinese Wilson'

A young member of staff at Kew Gardens, London, E. H. Wilson (1876–1930) was selected to undertake a journey to China to find the 'Handkerchief Tree'. He found it and a great many more plants. His sponsors, Veitch & Sons of Chelsea, London, sent him a second time. He undertook two more expeditions to China, but this time for the Arnold Arboretum, of Boston, U.S.A. From China he brought back four montanas – *rubens, wilsonii, grandiflora* and *spooneri*. The first, though, had already been found by Augustine Henry and the third by Nathaniel Wallich. But Wilson brought them into cultivation. *C. spooneri* as far as we know is lost. Altogether Wilson introduced thirteen clematis to cultivation. After more explorations for Boston, Wilson succeeded his friend, Sargant, as Curator of the Arnold Arboretum. He died prematurely in 1930 in a car accident, which also killed his wife.

PLATE 137.
A single flower of 'Wilsonii' with its distinctive long stamens.

PLATE 138.
'Wilsonii'- leaf form.

Identifying Your Clematis

As related in Chapter I, the gardener can think of the montana group as sub-divided into three sub-groups:

I	Montanas – main sub-group	e.g. 'Rubens'
II	Chrysocoma – small sub-group -	e.g. 'Continuity'
III	Vedrariensis – small sub-group -	e.g. 'Rosea '

In a particular garden there may be variation from the standard colour for that montana for a number of reasons. A montana on the market may have been produced from a clone slightly different from the usual. The position of a plant in or out of sun can affect its colour; the more sun the more colour. The quality of the soil can affect the colour of a bloom giving more or less colour. The climate in which the garden lies can affect colour; a sombre climate leads to less colour. The time in the life of a bloom at which the judgement of colour is made can affect outcome; the younger the bloom the more colour. Here the judgement is made just after the bud opens to a full bloom.

I. The Montanas sub-group

In identifying plants in the main montana sub-group the most significant item in comparison is that of colour. This leads to dividing this group according to whether it is white, pale pink, pink, dark pink. The most difficult groups to tell apart are the 'pale pinks' and the 'pinks'.

A significant distinction can be made by whether the flower is single or double. Thus they will be treated separately here.

In addition to whether the flower is single or double and its colour, significant other factors to consider are its size and shape, whether it is scented or not, size and foliage of the plant and time of flowering. The gardener can easily identify all the plants if they are judged on the above criteria.

The related white clematis *C. gracilifolia* is included in this group.

PLATE 139.
(Clockwise) 'Grandiflora', *C. gracifolia*, 'White Fragrance' and *C. montana*.

White single Montanas

There are six:–
1. *C. montana*; 2. 'Alexander'; 3. *C. gracilifolia*; 4. 'Grandiflora' and
5. 'White Fragrance'. In addition there is 6. *C. wilsonii* which flowers much later than the others and will be treated separately.

Four of these are illustrated above in Plate 139.

Large 'Grandiflora' dominates and, clockwise from it, there is *C. gracilifolia*, 'White Fragrance' and *C. montana*.
'Grandiflora' has a large bloom, the tepals overlap and it has very little scent. It is on an enormous plant, the foliage is not distinctive and it flowers with the main group. Distinctive features – large bloom on a large plant.
C. gracilifolia has a small flower, the tepals overlap, it has no scent, is on a moderate-sized plant and the foliage is distinctive. It also flowers early. Distinctive feature is dark greyish-green foliage that may be pinnate.
'White Fragrance' has a small flower, its shape is irregular, it is heavily scented on a large plant, the foliage is not distinctive and it flowers towards the end of the flowering of the main group. Distinctive feature is irregular-shaped flower.
C. montana is a small, star-shaped flower, scented, on a large plant without distinctive foliage and flowers with the main group. Distinctive feature is small star-shaped flower.

PLATE 140.
'Alexander' with its distinctive 'cupped' flower shape.

'Alexander' could not be included with the above as it failed to flower this year. 'Alexander' is a small flower, it is slightly 'cupped' and has wavy margin to the tepals. It has no scent, the plant is of a moderate size, the foliage is not distinctive and it flowers early. It is scented and the colour is creamy-white, flecked with green. (See Plate 140.) Distinctive feature is the 'cupped' shape of flower.

PLATE 141.
C. wilsonii is a distinctive flower with long stamens and notched petals.

C. wilsonii flowers two months later than the other white clematis. (See Plate 141.) Distinctive features are the white blooms with many long stamens and thick, notched, pointed tepals.

PLATE 142.
'Pink Perfection', 'Elizabeth' and 'Odorata'.

Pale pink single Montanas

Here there are three clematis to be considered: 'Pink Perfection', 'Elizabeth' and 'Odorata'. They are seen in that order in Plate 142, looking from left to right. Plate 143 compares 'Odorata' on the left with 'Elizabeth' on the right.

PLATE 143.
'Odorata' on the left, 'Elizabeth' on the right.

'Odorata' is much smaller than 'Elizabeth', both are deeply scented and both make large plants. They flower at about the same time. Distinctive feature of 'Odorata' is the small, much scented flower.

PLATE 144.
'Elizabeth' on the left is compared with 'Pink Perfection'.

Plate 144 compares 'Elizabeth' with 'Pink Perfection'. They make flowers of about the same size. There is more colour in 'Elizabeth'. The colour in 'Pink Perfection' is suffused or central. In 'Elizabeth' the colour concentrates towards the edge. 'Pink Perfection' has broader overlapping tepals. The tepals in 'Elizabeth' may recurve. Both are deeply scented. 'Elizabeth' has the darker leaf. A distinctive feature of 'Elizabeth' is the colour concentrated at the edge of the tepal. The distinctive feature of 'Pink Perfection' is the colouring concentrated centrally in the tepal.

PLATE 145.
(Top row, left to right) 'Mayleen', 'Gothenburg', 'Vera', and 'Lilacina'.
(Bottom row, left to right) 'Rubens', 'East Malling', 'Fragrant Spring' and 'Olga'.

Pink single Montanas
Eight have to be considered. (See Plate 145.) From left to right, top row: 'Mayleen', 'Gothenburg', 'Vera' and 'Lilacina'. From left to right, bottom row: 'Rubens', 'East Malling', 'Fragrant Spring' and 'Olga'.

'Mayleen' has a large flower. The broad tepals overlap. It has a strong scent. It grows on a very large plant. Its foliage is mid-green. It flowers with the main group. Distinctive features are the broad tepals.

'Gothenburg' has a large flower. The flower is 'cupped'. It is slightly scented. It grows on a medium-sized plant. The foliage is characteristic having a silver line down the leaflets. It flowers with the main group. Distinctive feature is the foliage.

'Vera' has a large flower which is 'gappy' and has strong scent. It grows on a large plant. The foliage is mid-green. It flowers with the main group. Distinctive feature is the large 'gappy' bloom.

'Lilacina' is a medium-sized flower. The tepals often recurve. There is slight scent. It grows on a medium-sized plant. The foliage is mid-green and it flowers with the main group. It has a lilac tinge to the pink. The distinctive feature is the lilac tinge. (bottom line, from left to right)

'Rubens' has a large flower and the tepals do not overlap. It is highly-scented. It grows on a medium-sized plant. The foliage is bronzy. It flowers with the main group. Distinctive feature is the bronzy foliage.

'East Malling' has a small flower. The tepals overlap and recurve at tip. It is scented, it grows on a huge plant, the foliage is light green and it flowers with the main group. Distinctive feature is vigour of plant.

'Fragrant Spring' has a small flower, there is no overlap of tepals. It is highly scented. It grows on a medium-sized plant. The foliage is characteristic, being bronzy, with many of the leaf margins uncut. It flowers with the main group. Distinctive feature is the foliage.

'Olga' has a medium-sized bloom. The tepals are round, making a tidy bloom. It has scent. It grows on a medium-sized plant. The foliage is characteristic, being purple. It flowers with the main group. The distinctive feature is the foliage.

PLATE 146.
'Mayleen' and 'Vera'.

The large blooms of 'Mayleen' and 'Vera' could be confused. However, a glance at the flowers makes the distinction very clear. (See Plate 146.) 'Mayleen', on the right, has tepals that overlap. In 'Vera' the tepals do not overlap and the flower is 'gappy'.

PLATE 147.
'Rubens' and 'East Malling'.

'Rubens' and 'East Malling' could be confused. (See Plate 147) 'Rubens', on the left, has more colour and has more scent. It also has bronzy foliage – on the left, in Plate 148, while 'East Malling' has light green foliage – on the right of the plate.

PLATE 148.
(Left to right) 'New Dawn', 'Veitch', 'Freda' and 'Warwickshire Rose'.

Single dark pink Montanas
Here we have to consider six plants: 'Freda', 'New Dawn', 'Picton's Variety' 'Tetrarose', 'Veitch' and 'Warwickshire Rose'. Four are depicted from left to right on Plate 148 – 'New Dawn', 'Veitch', 'Freda' and 'Warwickshire Rose'. ('Tetrarose' and 'Picton's Variety' were not available for this plate but will be considered separately in Plates 149 and 150.)

'New Dawn' has a medium-sized flower, a little 'cupped' in shape. It has slight scent in mature bloom. It grows on a medium-sized plant. The foliage is bronzy and it flowers with the main crop of Montanas. Distinctive feature is the 'cupped' bloom.

'Veitch' makes a small flower. It is highly coloured. There is slight scent in mature flower. It grows on a small plant. The foliage is bronzy and it flowers with the main crop. Distinctive feature is the small highly-coloured bloom.

'Freda' has a medium-sized bloom. The colour of the flower is two-toned. It has slight scent in the mature flower. It grows on a small plant. The foliage is deep bronze. It flowers early. Distinctive features are two-toned bloom and dark foliage.

'Warwickshire Rose' has a small flower. It is deeply coloured. It has no scent. It grows on a large plant. The foliage is very dark. It flowers with the main crop. Distinctive feature is the very dark foliage.

PLATE 149.
'Tetrarose'.

'Tetrarose' is a large-sized flower of clear pink colour. The concave tepals do not overlap. It has slight scent in mature bloom. It grows on a medium-sized plant. The foliage is bronzy. It flowers with the main crop. (See Plate 149.) Distinctive feature is the large, deep-pink flower.

PLATE 150.
'Picton's Variety'.

'Picton's Variety' has a medium-sized flower. The four–six tepals only slightly overlap. There is deep pink colour. There is spicy scent. It grows on a small plant. The foliage is bronzy. It flowers with the main crop. Distinctive feature is the very pink flower and spicy scent. (See Plate 150.)

PLATE 151.
(Left to right) 'Pleniflora', 'Margaret Jones' and 'Jacqui'.

Double white Montanas
Here we have to consider three clematis 'Pleniflora', 'Margaret Jones' and 'Jacqui'. They are found in Plate 151, from left to right.

'Pleniflora' has a small flower. This in the bud stage points upwards. It has points on the ends of its tepals. Later blooms are double. It has no scent. The foliage is mid-green. It flowers with the main crop. Distinctive feature is the upward pointing open bell as the bud opens.

'Margaret Jones' has a small flower. This is often creamy-green at first, turning creamy-white. It has no scent. It is on a medium-sized plant. The foliage is mid-green. It flowers towards the end of the flowering of the main group. Distinctive feature is the creamy-green or creamy-white irregular flower.

'Jacqui' has the largest flower. It has stamens. Many of the flowers are double. The staminoides are often flushed pink in mature flower. It has no scent. It is on a small plant. Foliage is mid-green. It flowers with the main crop. The distinctive feature is the presence of stamens.

PLATE 152.
'Broughton Star' and 'Marjorie'.

Non-white doubles

Here we have to consider 'Broughton Star' on the left and 'Marjorie' on the right of Plate 152. The distinction here is clear. 'Broughton Star' is the larger flower and the hues are red. 'Marjorie' is a smaller flower and the hues here are yellow and pink.

PLATE 153.
C. Chrysocoma and 'Continuity'.

PLATE 154.
C. Chrysocoma and 'Rosea'.

II The Chrysocoma Sub-Group

Here we have to consider two clematis, *C. chrysocoma* on left and 'Continuity' on the right of Plate 153. 'Continuity' has the larger flower. The flower in *C. chrysocoma* is cupped while the flower in 'Continuity' is open. Neither has scent. Both are on medium-sized plants. The foliage of both is dark. They flower later than the montanas. The outstanding difference is the greater colour in 'Continuity' and its marvellous stamens.

C. chrysocoma on the left, may need to be distinguished from 'Rosea' on the right in Plate 154. Both flowers are slightly cupped. 'Rosea' has more colour. Neither has scent. Both grow on medium- sized plants but there is a distinct difference in foliage. Foliage of 'Rosea' is very bronzy on the left in Plate 155, while that of *C. chrysocoma* on right is dark-green.

PLATE 155.
Compare the bronzy foliage of 'Rosea' on the left with that of *C. Chrysocoma* which is dark green.

PLATE 156.
(Left to right) 'Hidcote', 'Highdown' and 'Rosea'.

III The Vedrariensis Sub-Group

Group III, Vedrariensis, came from crossing of Groups I and II and have some of the characteristics of both Group I and Group II.

Here we have to consider 'Hidcote', 'Highdown' and 'Rosea', from left to right in Plate 156.

'Hidcote' has an open flower, rather like a montana. It is scented. It makes a big plant. The foliage is light-green. It is the earliest to flower of the Vedrariensis. There is no bronze in the foliage.

'Highdown' has a cupped flower. It has no scent. It makes a big plant. The foliage is dark-green with some bronze.

'Rosea' has a 'cupped' flower. It is the deepest pink. It has no scent. It makes a small plant. Its foliage is very bronzy and very distinctive.

CHAPTER IV
SUPPLEMENTARY LIST OF MONTANAS

The gardener, to whom this book is directed, requires plants that are proven garden worthy. However worthy a plant, if it is not commercially available, then it is of no use to him. The list below consists of both categories – plants not completely evaluated and plants not yet generally available. However, inclusion on this list is in no way a down-grading of a plant. On the contrary, some of these plants will be the successes of the future.

Listed also are plants from the wild related to the montanas, not yet commercially available. Finally, there is a short list of lost montanas.

PLATE 157.
Bi-color.

PLATE 158.
Bi-color.

EUROPE

'Bi-color'

Acquired by Logan Botanic Garden, Port Logan, near Stranraer, Scotland, before 1974. Origin unknown. Listed Edinburgh Botanic Garden, 1974 (4306). Introduced by Northern Liners Ltd., U.K. in 2003. Pink and white tepals change over a short time to clear white. Heavily scented. Deep green attractive leaves. Strong plant. Very promising introduction.

'Brookfield Clove'

Raised by Treasures of Tenbury, U.K. from material that came from Stuart Brookfield of Cannington, Somerset, U.K. Available since 2002. Pink tepals marked 'like old carnations'. Clove scent.

'Christine'

From a seedling from a seed exchange, selected and raised by Sheila Chapman of Sheila Chapman Nursery, Abingford, Essex, UK, and named after her daughter. This newcomer can be regarded as an improved 'Grandiflora'. It has attractive 'pinking' on the bud and also mauvy-pink edging to the back of the white tepals. It greatly improves on 'Grandiflora', which only has a slight scent, by very strong fragrance. Grown in a container, I also noticed that it made a larger flower than 'Grandiflora', large as that flower is. Available in 2005.

PLATE 159.
Christine.

PLATE 160.
C. Chrysocoma.

C. chrysocoma (dwarf)

This is the true chrysocoma plant and a most attractive dwarf. Described by Jack Elliot (The Clematis. 1993) from his observation at Lijiang in Western Yunnan as non-climbing and less than a metre high. Lobed leaves covered in golden hairs. Pale pink flowers. Described by Roy Lancaster (*Travels in China.* 1989.) Similarly with satiny-pink tepals. Flowers 5–6cm. (2–2½in.) across on long erect stalks. Found only in Yunnan, China. Grown in private gardens from introduced seed. Not yet commercially available. Pink of early flower fades to pale pink or white in mature flower.

'Dovedale' (syn. *C. x vedrariensis* 'Dovedale')

Raised by Barry Fretwell of Perivale Clematis Nursery, Christow, near Exeter, U.K. before 1950. A hybrid between *C. chrysocoma* and 'Picton's Variety'. Flower is six- or seven-tepaled; clear-pink; 7.5cm. (3in.) across. Central deeper pink bar in tepal. Foliage is red underneath, grows up to 4.5–6m. (15–20ft.).

PLATE 161.
Elten.

'Elten'

This new introduction from Germany has been described as a white 'Mayleen'. Named after the village of Elten, Germany, near the Dutch–German border. Habit is vigorous, hardy, floriferous. Flower is white with four broad obovate tepals. Prominent stamens; anthers – yellow; filaments – white. Pistil is prominent. On long stalks. Strong scent. Large leaved foliage is bronzy when young, light green later. May prove to be a splendid introduction.

PLATE 162.
'Sir Eric Savill'.

PLATE 163a.
'Sir Eric Savill'.

PLATE 163b.
Buds of 'Sir Eric Savill'.

'Sir Eric Savill'.
Named after the creator of the Savill Garden at Windsor, U.K. Introduced at the Savill Garden, Windsor, after 1951. Regarded as an improved version of 'Rubens'. Has more colour and a larger flower than 'Rubens' but less scent. The buds are handsome, being globular and covered completely in deep mauve-pink. Pinky-mauve tepals that are darker mauve-pink behind. Yellow anther, green connective. White filament. Pistil is green and prominent. Foliage is bronzy with brown stems. There is no fragrance, or it is very faint. Does not make a massive plant.

'Snow'
Listed in *Plantfinder* up to 1967.

'Superba'
A clematis under this name was introduced by George Jackman and Son of Woking, Surrey, U.K. before 1910. It was awarded an Award of Merit by the R.H.S. on 2 May 1914. It was described in *The Garden*, 1910. 74, 119; by William Robinson in *The Garden*, 1914, 78, 270; in *The Garden Chronicle*, 1914, 287; in *The Gardener's Magazine* in 1914, p.370 and in the J.R.H.S. 1915–1916. p.LXVIII. It was a hybrid from 'Grandiflora' x 'Mrs George Jackman'. It may be the plant described by Christopher Lloyd on p.71 of his book *Clematis* which he found wanting and which was also withdrawn by Jackman's.

From the above references it is clear that 'Superba' had white flowers and should not be confused with a pink version of 'Rubens' in circulation under the same name and of uncertain origin. The white flower is the subject of a painting by Magnus Johnson on p.34 of his *Slaktet Klematis*. I understand it is re-introduced from Sweden and is now available. (Picture unavailable).

PLATE 164.
'Unity'.

PLATE 165.
'Yuishan'.

'Unity'
A chance seedling, probably from 'Elizabeth', at the nursery of Sheila Chapman, Abridge, Essex, U.K. Introduced in 2001 and named after the mother of the raiser. It can be regarded as an improved version of the desirable 'Elizabeth'. It was called 'Big Lizzy' by the raiser at first. The flower is larger than in 'Elizabeth'. Has larger lighter leaves and is even more intensely perfumed. I was impressed with it in a container but have yet to estimate its garden performance which could be stunning.

C. x vedrariensis
Its name stands for the Latin for 'From Verrieres', France. Sometimes wrongly called *C. spooneri* or *C. spooneri* 'Rosea'. Messrs. Vilmorin-Andrieux at Verrières-le-Buisson near Paris, France, had received seed of *C. chrysocoma* from Abbé Delavay. They crossed 'Rubens' with *C. chrysocoma* in 1911 and plants flowered in 1913. The result was shown to the National Horticultural Society of France in 1914. It is said to have the habit of 'Rubens' and the downiness of *C. chrysocoma*. It is less vigorous than *C. montana*. 'Good pink colour' – (Christopher Lloyd).

   Photographs in *Garden Chronicle*, 55, 392; *Garden Chronicle*, 61, 94, 3 March 1917 and *J.R.H.S.* 67, 1941, Fig.118. Award of Merit, R.H.S., 9 June 1936. The report states: 'blush-pink' colour; 5cm. (2in.) across; from Mr Ernest Markham.

   Not often available. In this sub-group 'Highdown' and 'Rosea' are more popular.

'Yuishan' (Jade Mountain)
Collected by Bleddyn and Sue Wynne-Jones of Crug Farm Plants, Caernarvon, North Wales, at altitude of 3,400m. (10,000ft.) on Taiwan's highest mountain and named after it. Introduced 2002. Single. White flowers. Yellow anthers. Flowers profusely. Climbs up to 6m. (20ft.)

AUSTRALIA

In her book *Growing Clematis: A Complete Guide*, Bridget Gubbin writes of two montana-like clematis – **'Arguta'** and **'Rhamnoides'**.

'Arguta'
Name stands for 'sharp toothed'. The author describes the flowers as creamy, with four tepals and similar to a smaller Montana. The leaves are reminiscent of the Montanas.

'Rhamnoides'
The name stands for 'like Buckthorn'. Found by camellia collector, Bob Withers. Single flowers opening very flat. Four clear pale pink tepals with rounded ends. Lime-green stamens. Plant has a slight scent. The leaves suggest a cross between *C. chrysocoma* and *C. montana*. Plant has a slightly suckering habit. Climbs to 1 metre (3¼ feet).

'Wrightii'
Des Mumford of Gippsland Growers, Warragul, Australia, describes a montana in *The Clematis*, 1994, p.87: "One of my favourites is *C. montana* 'Wrightii' which is similar in appearance to *C. montana rubens*, but with foliage that is more deeply serrated. *C. montana* 'Wrightii' is a far less vigorous growth that *C. montana rubens* but has a larger, deeper, rose pink, single flower, similar to C. 'Tetrarose' from a distance. It also flowers slightly later than *C. montana rubens*. Breeder and origin unknown.

PLATE 166.
Jenny Keay.

NEW ZEALAND

'Jenny Keay'
A new double white clematis is always welcome. This comes from a renowned nursery at Christchurch, New Zealand. Named after wife of raiser. Propagated by nurseryman Merv Jerard and raised by Alexander Keay at his nursery in Christchurch, New Zealand. First flowered in 1991. Introduced in 1996. Attractive semi-double and double flowers. 4.5cm. (1⅘in.) across. Four white tepals and two–three layers of greeny-white pistil. No fragrance. Foliage is ternate, small, mid-green with irregularly-toothed leaflets.

The Mitchell Hybrids
Robin Mitchell supplied the following introduction to this unique venture:

"The *C. montana* group cultivars announced by Robin and Lorna Mitchell mostly – or possibly, all – derive from a chance seedling brought by them from their former property when they moved house in 1989. The seedling was sufficiently different from the traditional varieties to be referred to Bayliss Nurseries Ltd. who propagated and marketed it, leaving the Mitchells to proceed with a breeding programme – a pattern which still exists, except that overseas marketing is now by Growell Plants of Waitara, North Island.

"The original cultivar, 'Starlight', has been superseded by 'Starlight Improved', and both have been crossed with traditional varieties to produce the large number of new cultivars now listed. Of recent years the crossing has been haphazard, with seedlings selected pre-flowering for vegetative characteristics and culled at flowering if the flowers are not found desirable. A possible exception to 'Starlight' parentage is the cultivar 'Giant Star', which seems more related to 'Tetrarose', perhaps as a mutant. The crossings are encouraged by planting established varieties alongside – mostly of *C. montana* group but including members of *C. alpina* and *C. macropetala*, though there seems no evidence of hybridisation with these other groups."

131

PLATE 167.
'Apricot Star'.
Introduced 2002.
Semi–double. Pinkish
apricot.

PLATE 168.
'Crinkle'.
Introduced in 1997.
Single. Deep pink.

PLATE 169.
'Doctor Penelope'.
Named 2000. Single.
Cream.

PLATE 170.
'Dusky Star.'
Named 1999. Double.
Pink.

PLATE 171.
'El Pinko'.
Introduced 2001.
Single. Pink.

PLATE 172.
'Frilly Pants'.
Named 2000. Single.
Pinky-white.

PLATE 173.
'Giant Star'.
Named in 1997.
Single. Mid-pink.

PLATE 174.
'Joyful Star'.
Named 2002.
Double. Pink and
white. Scented.

PLATE 175.
'Magic Star'.
Named 1966.
Double. Pink.

PLATE 176.
'Pink Starlight'.
Named 1998.
Semi-double. Pink.

PLATE 177.
'Pink Rave'.
Named 2000.
Single. Pink.

PLATE 178.
'Primrose Star'.
Introduced 1991.
Double. Pale
yellow.

PLATE 179.
'Rosebud'.
Named in
1997. Double.
Mid-pink.
Scented.

PLATE 180.
'Shirley Star'.
Named 2002.
Semi-double.
Pink.

'Starlet'.
(Unillustrated)
Named 2001.
Semi-double.
Yellow and
pink.

PLATE 181.
'Sweet
Mystery'.
Named 2001.
Single. White
and pink.
Scented.

PLATE 182.
'Starlight'.
Named 1900. Cream.
Slight scent.

PLATE 183.
'Sunrise'.
Introduced 1998. Single.
Deep-pink. Slightly
scented.

'Wee Willie Winkie'.
(Unillustrated)
Named 2001. Single.
Pink and white bicolour.

PLATE 184.
'White Rosebud'.
Named 2001. Semi–
double. White.

PLATE 184a.
'Snowflake'.

JAPAN

'Snowflake'.
The tepals are yellowish-white and anthers are greenish-yellow. 6–8cm. (2¼–3¼in.) across flower. Not fragrant. Can make a large plant. Possibly seedling of 'Grandiflora'. Introduced before 1986.

Mr Y. Aihara, who kindly supplied the information below, comments that montanas have a small place in clematis growing in Japan as their habit does not fit well into Japanese cultural practices.

From Mr Hayakawa:

'Hakuju'.
Single. White. Scented.

'Green Eye'.
Semi-double. White-green.

'Senju'.
Pink.

'Hakurakuten'.
White.

138

PLATE 184b.
'Hakuju'.

PLATE 184c.
'Green Eye'.

PLATE 184d.
'Senju'.

PLATE 185.
'Brewster', originally from the U.S.A.

U.S.A.

'Brewster'
A seedling found by Brewster Rogerson, Hillsboro, Oregon, U.S.A., who raised it. Named by Pacific Northwest Clematis Society in his honour. Registered by that society. Tepals a rich rose-pink with rose bar behind. Yellow anthers. Stems bronze-red. Up to 7m. (23ft.).

WILD

A group of plants related to the montanas mentioned by collectors as suitable for cultivation and may be introduced to gardens in time.

C. acerifolia – (bitter tasting leaves).
Related to montanas with palmate leaves. C. Grey-Wilson, (*Clematis. The Genus.* 2000.) regards it as worthy of cultivating.

C. brevipes – (short stems).
Creamy-white or yellowish-white flower on a plant not too dissimilar to *C. gracilifolia*. Thought to be worthy of cultivation by C. Grey-Wilson (*Clematis. The Genus.* 2000).

C. glabrifolia – (glabrous smooth leaves).
White flower. May already have been cultivated as it is listed as having appeared in a coloured lithograph in the nineteenth century.

C. tongluensis
Noted favourably by Roy Lancaster (*Plant Hunting in Nepal.* 1981), by Ludlow and Shereiff (*Quest of Flowers*) and Christopher Grey-Wilson (*Clematis. The Genus.* 2000.)

PLATE 186.
'C. tongluensis'.

C. trichogyna – M. C. Chang
Name means 'hairy ovaries'. White flowers with mucronate (tipped) tepals. Scented. Hardy. Cultivated by Magnus Johnson.

C. venusta – M. C. Chang
Name means 'graceful'. White elliptical tepals with wavy margin and recurved apex. Well regarded by Christopher Grey-Wilson *Clematis. The Genus.* 2000.)

LOST MONTANAS

C. anemoniflora
This term was used by David Don for 'montana' in his *Prodramus Florae Nepalensis* and published in 1825. Plant named 'montana' by its collector, Francis Buchanan and this name taken by De Candolle in his *Systema* of 1818. De Candolle's term had precedence and Don's term discarded.

Montanas from Lemoine
C. perfecta, C. undulata
See Historical Notes.

C. montana var. *wilsonii* f. *platysepala*
See Historical Notes.

C. Spooneri
See Historical Notes.

Chapter V
Cultivation of the Montanas

Introduction

The garden care of the montana group is easy. The plants are vigorous, predictable, and have an urge to grow. They will almost grow without any special care but of course do better if they receive it. All this, if the climate is right.

Everything about the montanas is easy – planting, pruning, control of diseases and propagation. They make just three demands – they must be kept well watered as they are large plants, they relish good feeding – again because they make massive growth within the course of a year, and the climate must be suitable. Given the right climate the only complaint of a gardener is usually that they grow too well! The montanas come from areas of thin soil in the mountain of India, Nepal and China. In the soil of our gardens dwarfs become giants.

Know Your Climate

Cultivation of the montanas turns around climate. In average conditions they are spectacular but they are sensitive to cold climates; special care in such climates can overcome the liability to fail.

One approach is to consider climate in terms of latitude. However, so many other factors are involved, such an approach can be over simple. A more useful approach defines climatic zones in terms of the lowest annual temperature in a territory. This approach has been worked out in the United States and produces a complex pattern that does not coincide just with the pattern based on latitude. Factors additional to latitude and temperature in a territory are: 1) Height above or below sea-level; 2) the maritime status – close or far from the sea; 3) the relative pattern of oceanic currents; 4) the rainfall and snowfall; 5) the pattern of prevailing winds; 6) forestation; 7) sunshine rates, and 8) direction of prevailing wind. The table, published later (p.144), establishes that montanas need an area with a winter temperature of not lower than −18°C (0°F) and they can be grown in Zones 7–9 of the American zones.

Having established your zone you still need to consider the micro-climate of your garden. Despite being in the right zone for growing montanas you may find deficiencies in your garden that will make it difficult to grow montanas. On the contrary, you may find unexpected assets in your garden that will make it easy to grow montanas. Methods of protecting plants, to be discussed later, may also make it possible for you to proceed in an unfavourable climate. Growth takes place when the temperature rises over 6°C (43°F). Temperature is greatest at soil level. Temperature changes decrease with depth of soil and disappear at a depth of 10cm. (4in.). A soil depth of only 5cm. (2in.) can make a big difference in temperature. Certain clematis can be grown on a south-facing wall in the northern hemisphere but cannot be grown on a north-facing wall. The reverse applies in the southern hemisphere. Again, an east wall gets sun first and if a plant has frozen in the night, it is likely to be damaged by a thaw. Slopes facing south are warm and in a dell, out of the wind, it may be possible to grow clematis that would be damaged on an exposed site. By contrast, however, a dell with no passage of air can become a frost pocket. The height of the garden above sea-level can make a dramatic difference from similar gardens nearby not in elevated positions. Surprisingly small differences in the height make enormous differences in cultivation. The volcanic island of Madeira is a lesson in this connection: for every 100m. (250ft.) rise in height the temperature falls by 0.5°C (1°F).

Check, therefore, your zone and see if you can improve on it by adjusting the micro-climate of your garden or taking special measures of winter protection.

A Garden Plan

Labels have a life of their own. They break, they become indistinct and they disappear. Thus it is essential to have a plan of the garden which clearly shows the position of each montana. This can be part of an already existing garden plan. Otherwise it can be created just for the clematis.

It is useful to divide the garden into sections giving each a name – for example, 'the oval bed', 'the north bed', 'the long bed', etc. Each section can have a page of the plan to itself. A particular mark such as an 'X' can indicate the position of a montana. To each mark add the name of the montana clematis.

To make it easy, and to recognise instantly the position of a clematis, it is useful to mark on the plan permanent structures such as posts, trees, or marks on the walls. The permanent structures are named on the plan. The positions of the montana clematis are related on the plan to these permanent structures and it makes the clematis easy to find.

The plan will be invaluable in the winter when the time comes to plan new plantings for the following year. Indeed, it is possible to mark further positions for more clematis on the plan with broken crosses. See sample plan. (Fig. IV).

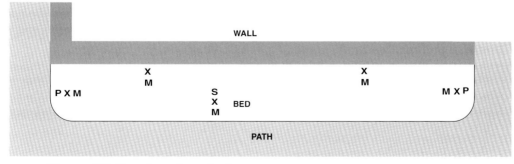

Figure IV. Planning a long bed.
(M= Montana, P= Post, S= Shrub, X= Planting Position.)

Planting

Experienced Gardeners

For you it will be very simple. Just plant a montana as you would any other of your shrubs (I will provide more detail for the less experienced gardener).

Planning

Plan your planting some time beforehand. Consult your garden plan and decide where a montana can be planted with advantage. In the case of spring

planting, time can be devoted to the planning during the winter. Indeed the holes can be prepared during the winter for spring planting. It is said that an hour's gardening in winter is as good as five hours in the summer!

The main planting of montanas should be in the spring. At this time the soil is warming up and the plant has an urge to grow. The second best time is in the early autumn allowing the plant to be established before winter and in favourable climates to make some root growth in the winter. However, as long as the ground is not frozen, the montana can be planted, if in a pot, at any time of the year.

Buying your Montana

Clematis are sold in three styles:
1. A mature two year-old plant, usually in a 2-litre pot, that can be put into the ground right away. (See Plate 187). This is the commonest style.

How do you tell a good plant? Firstly, look at the foliage. Are the leaves clean and healthy looking? Check the bottom of the pot. Are the roots visible through the bottom hole? If so, that is a good sign. If in doubt ask the staff to tip the plant out of the pot. You can now check the roots. Are there any insects or larvae on the roots? If so reject the plant. Being 'pot bound' is not often a problem with clematis.

PLATE 187.
A mature plant.

2. A first year plant is termed a 'liner' in the trade (See Plate 188). They can be just as healthy as a mature plant but they need another year before they can be planted. They have the advantage of being much cheaper but you wait longer for the bloom. To these you must do two things:

a) Repot in a 15.5cm. (6½in.) diameter pot. Use a good compost. If in doubt use John Innes No.3. Mix a teaspoonful of long-acting fertiliser or a small lump of a long-acting fertiliser – but keep well away from the centre of the plant. Fit pot with a 1m. (3ft.) cane. Where will you put this plant? If you have a greenhouse you can keep it there for a year but a better place for it is in the ground. At a sheltered corner of the garden sink it into the ground with soil up to and covering the top edge. It will be snug there until mature enough to plant. Only in very dry periods need you water it. Do not water it at all in the winter. As it makes long stems tie them to the cane. These long stems can also be pruned to above their first node; in this way you strengthen your montana. Do not worry about producing flowers during this year, concentrate instead on making a strong plant.

PLATE 188.
A liner.

PLATE 189.
Node.

b) Prune the plant. Prune by cutting the stem or stems above the node nearest to the ground. The node is the bump on the stem where leaves emerge. This will have the effect of stimulating the plant to throw up more stems from the crown and so make a stronger plant.

3. Increasingly clematis are being sold as plugs (See Plates 190-191). They seem to stand delivery by the postal services very well. Again, they are immature plants, not yet ready to be planted. They have the advantage, like a liner, of being cheap but need to be looked after for a year. Plant in a 16.5cm. (6½in.) pot and let it settle for six weeks. Prune as with a 'liner' and then put pot into the ground for a year, or until root system fills the pot and the plant is strong. Care for it as with 'liners'.

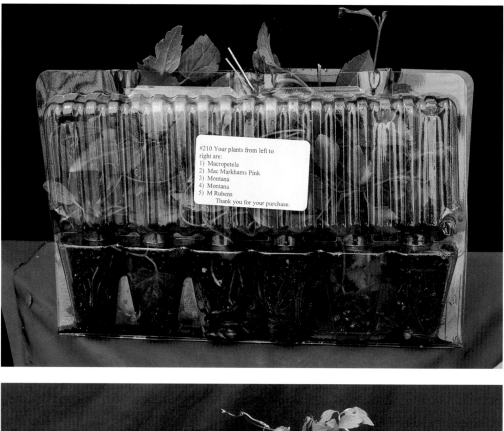

#210 Your plants from left to
right are:
1) Macropetela
2) Mac Markhams Pink
3) Montana
4) Montana
5) M Rubens
    Thank you for your purchase.

PLATES 190-191.
Plants as plugs.

Sources for plants

The first point of purchase for many plants is the internet. Contact my website (www.howells98.freeserve.com.uk) for a list of nurseries. You can approach the website of specialist nurseries in Holland, Germany, France, Japan, U.S.A. and the U.K. For lists of plants and supplying nurseries, contact PLANTFINDER (www.rhs.org.uk) also PPP INDEX for Europe.

Many will visit a specialist clematis nursery. Often the owner developed an interest in the plant as a gardener, loves it and moved into growing and selling it. These nurseries know their clematis. Advice is possible but not of course a long lecture. There will be a large choice of plants but buy the one you decided at home that you needed or you will be the victim of 'impulse buying'. All the nurseries will have their own informative catalogues that you can study at home and they often have a display garden.

Garden centres often have a good choice of the most popular montanas although the choice will be less than that at a specialist nursery. Also they are less likely to have the unusual. Naturally, advice is likely to be more superficial than in the specialist nursery. Some nurseries and outlets sell 'liners' alone. These may be a satisfactory choice but be aware that you have the care of the plant for at least a year before you can put it out in the garden.

Your rights

Most countries will have laws that define the customer's rights. In the U.K. for intance, under the Sale of Goods Act 1979, all plants must:
1.   Fit their description, e.g. be correctly labelled.
2.   Be of merchantable quality, e.g. the clematis must be healthy.
3.   Be reasonably fit for their purpose, e.g. if the clematis was brought as suitable for a certain climate then it should be so.

Delivery

If you order by post then your montana will often be delivered in the autumn. It can be planted in early autumn. If it is late autumn there is much to be said for repotting the clematis into a larger pot, keeping it protected in a trench in the garden and planting it in the spring. It is now becoming more common for clematis nurseries to supply plants ready for planting in the spring. Container-grown clematis can be planted at any time during the year, if conditions are favourable.

Pruning of new clematis

It is a great advantage if the plant has more than one stem. If the plant has just one stem then prune the plant by cutting across the stem above the lowest node. From the node will come two stems that can be spread out. Additional stems may come from the crown. With a number of stems the plant can be spread over a large area. Also in old age the plant can be pruned a stem at a time.

Situation

Ideally montanas enjoy growing in full sun away from the wind, but are accommodating and will grow well in less than ideal situations. Montanas will grow in semi-shade and on north-facing walls in the right climatic areas.

Soil

The ideal soil is friable, well-drained, and loamy and planting in it becomes easy because it contains all the necessary conditions for a healthy plant. In practice gardeners do not find themselves with the ideal soil and it can be either too light or too heavy. Light soil is easy to work but water slips through it very quickly and it contains little nutriment. Such a soil needs the addition of humus in the form of manure, compost, peat or peat substitutes. A heavy soil may be full of nutrients but lacks drainage. Roots require not only water and nutriment but also oxygen. Oxygen will be absent if the roots are continually in water so care must be taken to drain the holes made for planting in such a heavy, clay soil. This can be done with broken brick or rubble to a depth of 10–15cm. (4–6in.). Clematis grow satisfactorily in soil which is neutral or acid.

The Hole

This should be large enough to take the roots of the montana comfortably without them being squeezed together. Clematis should have a hole of at least 45cm. (18in.) diameter and 60cm. (2ft.) deep.

When digging the hole mark out the area on the soil surface. Having removed the top layer with a spade, loosen the next layer with a fork before using the spade again to lift the soil out. Keep on loosening the soil with a fork to make your task much easier. Any soil that you discard put in the wheelbarrow and take away. (Keep good topsoil.) The commonest error is not to make the hole deep enough for clematis.

Proceed to plant the montana clematis like any other shrub. No special measures are required for the montanas. The area between the roots and the stems (the collar, neck or crown) should be 5cm. (2in.) below the surface. In very cold areas plant 10cm. (4in.) deep to give the crown of the plant extra winter protection. There is a view that clematis should be planted deep to assist management of stem rot (clematis wilt). As stem rot never damages a montana this advice is clearly inoperative.

It is useful to think of the plant hole in terms of five layers:

1. The bottom layer is where the roots will be growing. About 23cm. (9in.) is given to this layer to provide the roots with a good start. The roots require a rich medium for nourishment and also one which retains water. Use manure, compost or leaf mould with added fertiliser.

2. The second layer should be a mere 1cm. (½in.) of soil or peat. This is simply a barrier to keep the roots of the montana plant initially separate from the rich material below.

3. The third layer of about 23cm. (9in.) is where the clematis will be placed.

4. The fourth layer is above the clematis and extends to about 5cm. (2in.) as a blanket to the plant. In very cold areas this layer can be 10cm. (4in.).

The material in the third and fourth layers does not need to be as rich as the material in the bottom area and can consist of good topsoil taken out of the hole, or soil mixed with peat, leaf mould, compost or a sprinkling of slow release fertiliser. One handful of bonemeal may be added. Bonemeal should be avoided in light soils as it may attract ants and should be replaced by a general fertiliser.

5. The fifth layer is the lip area allowing 2cm. (1in.) below the soil level to make a saucer area into which water can gather either naturally or as the result of watering. Thus avoid leaving the soil convex at the top which encourages water to flow off.

The five layers are easily fitted into a 60cm. (2ft.) hole.

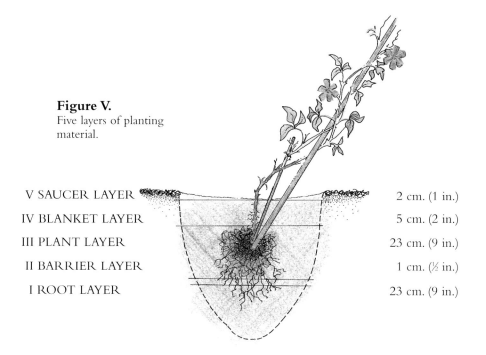

Figure V.
Five layers of planting material.

V SAUCER LAYER	2 cm. (1 in.)
IV BLANKET LAYER	5 cm. (2 in.)
III PLANT LAYER	23 cm. (9 in.)
II BARRIER LAYER	1 cm. (½ in.)
I ROOT LAYER	23 cm. (9 in.)

Order of Planting

Plants benefit from being immersed in water for a period of about two hours before planting to ensure that they have not dried out.

The montana can be extracted from its container by tapping the edge of the pot against the top of a fork or spade stuck into the ground or against a solid object. A thin plastic container should be cut open with care. Place the plant in the hole and replace the soil as directed above. Firm the material around the plant with your foot. If a cane is not attached to the clematis, mark the planting area with a short cane or stick which will prevent the montana from getting lost. Attach a label nearby. Montanas should be planted at good distances apart, at least 1.8m. (6ft.) or they will climb into one another and the strongest could kill the weakest!

Cane Support

The stems of the clematis plant usually arrive from the nursery attached to a cane. Ensure that the stems are firmly attached to the cane and, if need be, use new ties. This can help support the plant during planting and can carry the stem to a wall, post, host plant or other support if long enough. After planting you can insert a new cane in the ground and tie it to the original one to enable the plant to climb to its supporting shrub or structure.

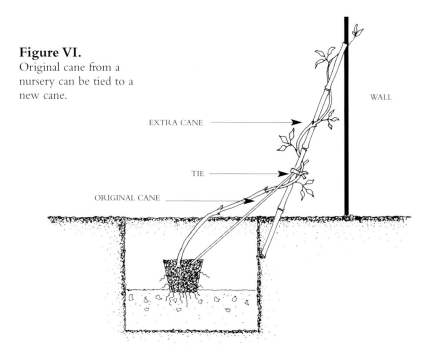

Figure VI.
Original cane from a nursery can be tied to a new cane.

WALL

EXTRA CANE

TIE

ORIGINAL CANE

Planting Near Walls

The soil near a wall is usually dry because rain may not reach it and the wall itself extracts water from the ground. Thus clematis should be planted at least 60cm. (2ft.) away from the wall. There are times, however, when it is not possible to do this and the clematis has to be planted very close to the wall. This can be successfully achieved if the plant is treated as if growing in a container, in which case excavate the old, poor soil and replace with new. Line the wall with slates or plastic sheeting to prevent the absorption of water. Great care must be taken to ensure that the area receives sufficient water: that is, 10 litres (2 gallons) of water per plant per week as a minimum. In hot weather it may be necessary to give 10 litres (2 gallons) of water each day. Furthermore attention should be paid to ensuring that plants do not dry out during the winter for the winter rain may not reach plants close to walls.

Planting into Trees

The hole for the montana must be far enough away from the tree trunk to guarantee plenty of good soil for root growth. Even several metres from the trunk creates no problems for the long stems of montanas. One plan advocates planting on the shady side of a tree so that light pulls the plant into the tree. But if there is too much shade the plant will make little growth. A better plan is to plant in good light and then guide the stems into the tree. Near the ground use canes. If the cane cannot reach into a tree, extend the cane by using thick string. Once one stem reaches the tree the rest will use that stem as a pathway to the tree. Once the stems are in a tree they can be guided upwards by tying stems to the branches with plastic ties. Exercise great care when using step-ladders and ladders. When out of your reach, the montana will take its own course – usually with brilliant results.

Moving Plants

Montanas should be moved from one part of the garden to another in the late autumn, winter or early spring when the soil is not frozen or waterlogged. In the case of large montanas, much of the top growth should be cut away to make the task manageable. A large well-established montana is unlikely to survive the moving.

Winter Protection

Cold temperatures can harm montanas in two ways: 1) the whole plant is killed. 2) the montana survives the winter, is in flower and a late frost kills all the buds, the plant remaining healthy.

Roots can be protected with a mulch of bark chippings, straw, leaves, peat, conifer prunings, crumpled paper, etc. to a depth of 15cm. (6in.) and covering the whole root area of the montana.

A simple method of protecting plants is to wrap the plant in a layer of horticultural fleece. Leave an exit for air above. Polythene bubble wrap is less successful as it does not breath and this encourages the development of grey rot, etc. In very cold areas use two layers of fleece. Leave fleece on the plant until there is no risk of frost. Fleece protection also encourages earlier flowering. To protect plant stems on a wall, hang a sheet of hessian sacking or fleece sheeting in front or hang netting in front of the plant and stuff it with insulating material. If a late frost is anticipated wrap small montanas with fleece or hang polythene sheeting in front of plant.

PLATE 192.
A polythene sheet combats frost.

PLATE 193.
Fleece protects a Montana.

If a plant looks as if all its stems have died in the winter do not cut it down immediately. Sometimes shoots appear low down on the plant later in the spring. The plant can be trimmed above these shoots and the new shoots given support.

Hot Climates

Montanas adjust well to hot climates but protect the crowns with thick mulch or plant them under paving. Give frequent and large amounts of water and ensure there is good drainage so that water does not stay as a pool around the roots. Plant in semi-shade when possible and protect from hot winds.

Regular Inspection

Newly planted montanas should be visited at least once a week. There may be signs of damage or early disease and these will respond best if treated promptly. Stems of montanas may need guiding in the best direction or may need tying in. Lack of water can be immediately remedied.

Period of Growth

A montana may take a number of years before it reaches its optimum height. It is fascinating to see the plant outgrowing the height of the previous year.

Labelling

The ideal label shows the name clearly, is easily visible, is permanent and yet not obtrusive. It is very difficult, with any label, to achieve all these requirements. The natural elements are very strong and can do severe damage to a label, even in one winter.

At the time of planting, the montanas should be labelled but the label should not be fixed on the plant. A clematis stem does not like the label attached to itself, especially if it is metal, and it may die. Also, labels attached to plants can disappear at the time of pruning! Thus the label should be attached to either the support of the montana or be put into the ground nearby. If the latter, they can impede hoeing and may be rendered invisible by weeds. Therefore a short wood or metal post may have to be fixed specially into the ground to support a label.

As has been said earlier, there are so many hazards with labels that it is imperative to have a plan showing the position of each montana. This plan can be consulted in the winter months and the correctness of the labels checked. Defective labels can then be put right for the growing season.

The most durable forms of labels tend to be the most expensive. The cheapest are the white or coloured plastic pieces with the name of the plant in so-called 'permanent' ink. Experience shows that a plastic piece becomes fragile after a season and the 'permanent' ink is hardly visible after two seasons at most. Thus it is necessary to replace most labels every year after checking with the plan of planting. White plastic labels do not add to the beauty of the garden and should be tucked out of sight. Horticultural suppliers, but not usually garden centres, now supply much thicker plastic labels which are much more durable but may still need to be over printed every year.

A Supply of Water

In theory it is possible to over-water; a hose directed continually at a piece of ground will ultimately leach all the nutrients out of it. This is unlikely to happen with the amount recommended here and in any event is likely to be counterbalanced by the rich feeding programme.

Montana clematis require a minimum of 5 litres (1 gallon) of water a week. The importance of giving clematis sufficient water cannot be overestimated. Montana clematis will take up to 20 litres (4 gallons) per plant per week and in hot weather will relish 5–10 litres (1–2 gallons) per plant per day.

To be sure that you can determine exactly how much water a plant is having it is best to direct the water specifically on to the plant rather than allow it to take its share from a general garden watering, i.e. spot watering.

Watering should take place out of the sun in the evenings. Watering will of course be assisted by having planted your montanas correctly with a saucer area at the top of the hole. The following methods of watering can be used:

1.   Watering can. It is hard work but it is easy to measure the amount each plant gets.
2.   By hose. If a hose is used then use a fine spray on both sides of the leaves.
3.   Generalised watering. Watering by using a sprayer.
4.   During planting, advantage can be taken to insert a watering tube into the soil. The aim is to lead the water straight to the root area. A pipe of 12cm. (4½in.) diameter and 38cm. (15in.) long will do the job. At the bottom end of the tube there should be a few stones to allow easy drainage. An alternative watering aid is to sink an empty plant pot close to the clematis and water through this. With this system put two-thirds of the water into the pipe or pot and the rest over the soil to keep moist any roots which are near to the surface. (See Figure VII).

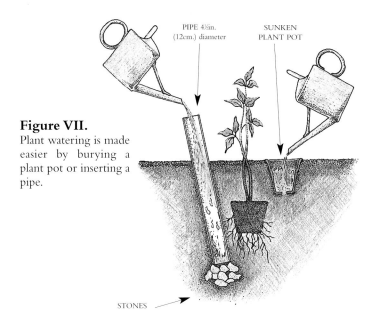

PIPE 4½in. (12cm.) diameter

SUNKEN PLANT POT

Figure VII.
Plant watering is made easier by burying a plant pot or inserting a pipe.

STONES

154

At the time of watering a liquid fertiliser can be given, either being dissolved in a watering can or being served from an attachment added to the hose.

The Best Watering System

The leaking, seeping or porous pipe systems are impressive and easy to install. Do a small area first and you will soon be accustomed to the fittings and method of installation. Once in place the saivng of time is enormous and quickly repays the cost and effort. The pipe can be put below the surface and the water goes to the exact spot that you planned to receive it, without wastage. It is easy to control the amount of water the plants receive, but make sure that the pipe is close, within centimetres, of your montana.

Large, well-established montanas will have a large root area and therefore are unbothered by short periods of drought. In a long drought, however, the montana will need watering.

Mulching

The main reason for using a mulch with montanas is to retain the moisture in the ground. This is much more effective than planting the roots in the shade or planting dwarf shrubs around the plant. Dwarf shrubs compete with the clematis for water and give little shade. Additional reasons for using a mulch are that it keeps the ground cool, it suppresses weeds, it adds humus to the ground and it will also help to add nutrients to the soil.

The mulch should be applied in the spring after the soil has warmed up. Remove any dead material from the ground and burn it. Later, inorganic or liquid fertilisers can be applied through it. The fertiliser should be watered in.

Apply sufficient mulch material to a thickness of at least 5–8cm. (2–3in.); 8–10cm. (3–4in.) will be even better. Do not carry the mulch material close to the stems as some of it, especially fresh manure, can damage them. (See Figure VIII.) A large montana may need to have a mulch covering several square feet. In the autumn the mulch material can be forked gently into the ground or left to protect the roots against severe weather.

Figure VIII.
The introduction of a thick layer of mulch (not less than 2ft. (60cm.) square around the clematis is beneficial. The material used should not come into contact with the plant stems.

The following material can be used:

1. Leaf mould contain some nutrients. It is usually acid. It is excellent mulching material.
2. Moist peat. This contains a little nitrogen only. It tends toward acidity and is therefore particularly good for alkaline soils.
3. Farmyard manure tends to be acid. Excellent mulching material but the manure must be old and in a state when it cuts like cake.
4. Garden compost. Tends to be acid. Excellent mulching material.
5. Well-rotted straw or sawdust.
6. Grass clippings. Effective but tend to take the nitrogen out of the soil. Should never be employed if a selected weed killer has been used on the lawn.
7. Pulverised bark. Contains few nutrients.
8. Mushroom compost. It is alkaline and therefore particularly good for acid soil. Mushroom compost has not usually been found to be satisfactory with clematis.
9. As a last resort stones, small bricks, or shingle can also be used.

An excellent method, and probably the one of choice, is covering the root area with porous sheeting. Porous sheeting prevents weeds coming through, retains water in the soil and, at the same time, being porous, allows water and fertilisers to pass easily through. Can be disguised with bark.

If materials which are liable to take nitrogen out of the soils are being used then 60–90 grams (2–3oz.) of sulphate of ammonia may be spread over the ground to 1 sq. m. (1 sq. yd.) before applying the mulch.

If clematis are planted in holes in stone material, as for example on a patio, then they will flourish exceedingly well because the stonework acts as a mulch. Naturally the soil in the hole must be well supplied with humus, nutrients, and water.

Feeding

In a good loamy soil little or no fertilising will be necessary but many soils do need feeding. Manure and garden compost give invaluable humus to the soil, improve drainage and the retention of water. Most energy must be given to the plants, however, in the form of fertilisers. These should be used according to recommended strength and spread evenly and uniformly about the plant and moved gently into the soil by fork or hand or hoe. Peat, although it contain no nourishment, is a good mulch and a soil conditioner. If used, it should be strengthened by containing an artificial fertiliser.

It is most important to ensure that manure, compost and artificial compost are spread well away from the stems of the plant – to a distance of 20cm. (8in.) Most of the roots are spread widely below and the fertiliser will reach them better away from the stem. Another important reason is that young manure and artificial fertiliser will rot the stems and even kill a plant. (See Figure IX)

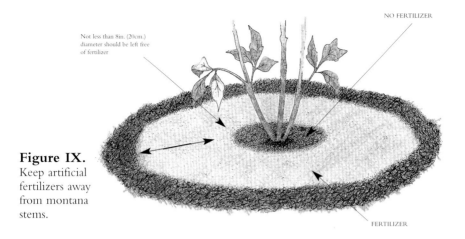

Figure IX.
Keep artificial
fertilizers away
from montana
stems.

Foliage feeding may be time-consuming but used once a week at recommended strength it is an excellent way of boosting your young montana plants. It is usually possible to undertake the foliar feeding with the watering programme.

Suggested Feeding Schedule

IN THE AUTUMN

Apply bonemeal at the rate of 100 grams (3½oz.) per sq. m. (per sq. yd.). Bonemeal is a slow-release fertiliser and will still be at work in the following spring and even longer. It tends to make the ground alkaline. It is rich with phosphates and encourages root growth. It should be worked gently into the ground. In light ground bonemeal may attract ants and should be replaced by a general fertiliser.

Provide a mulch of garden compost or well rotted manure, spreading it to about 60cm. (2ft.) around the plant. The manure must be well rotted and kept away from the stems.

IN THE SPRING

1. Gently dig in the autumn manure.
2. Apply a handful of potash or artificial fertiliser rich in potash. This encourages flower formation. Water it into the soil.
3. Now apply another mulch of suitable material.
4. If strong plants are required for a special reason, apply a liquid fertiliser, rich in potash, once a week. A well-established plant will enjoy the benefit of liquid feed twice a week. Never apply the fertiliser stronger than stated in the intructions; 'little and often' is the secret to success. Water first if the soil is dry. Stop the liquid fertiliser when the montana is in flower or it will shorten the flowering period.

157

IN MID-SUMMER

Give another handful of general fertiliser. Water it in.

PRUNING

Annual pruning of the montanas is unnecessary. A plant can exist for many years unpruned.

Some pruning is, however, indicated in the following special circumstances:

1. A plant spreading outside its allotted area. Montanas are such strong growers that inevitably they may stray outside the area you gave it leading, for example, to blocking garage doors, blocking pathways, obliterating a view from a window, crushing shrubs and small trees nearby, etc. (See Plate 194) The time to take action is AFTER flowering so that the impact it will make at that time is not impeded. Cut back the offending branches so that the plant now takes up less room than its allotted space. This will allow it to expand to just its allotted space by the end of the year. This cutting back will be required every year or every few years depending on circumstances.

PLATE 194.
'Time to prune' as it obscures a door.

2. Weakening in an old plant. The life of a montana is very long. Sometimes after twenty or even thirty years, the plant shows signs of weakening by producing fewer flowers and leaves.

Brave gardeners have been known to cut such plants down to within 1m . (3ft.) of the ground. It may work, but there is a considerable chance that the plant will die. A wiser course is to cut out one main branch this year, wait a year or two, then take out another main branch as the plant begins to respond to the pruning. At the same time help the plant by reviewing its water supply and reorganising this if required. Give the plant, over the wide area of its roots, a mulch of manure or compost and add a sprinkling of a general fertiliser over the whole area. This is done in the late spring after flowering.

3. Montanas sometimes overgrow their strength by going higher and higher into a tree. If weakening is appearing below, cutting away some of the higher growth can help the remaining plant. Again, this is undertaken in late spring after flowering.

DISEASES AND PESTS

There is no disease specific to the montanas. It does not suffer from stem rot (clematis wilt). It can, of course, be affected by the usual range of diseases and pests that afflict most plants.

The stems of the montanas can flop (wilt) in some circumstances but this is not due to stem rot of Phoma clematidina. Research has shown that while leaves of montanas can be invaded by the phoma, the plant has defences that prevent it entering the plant. Thus flopping (wilting) is always due to another cause – e.g. lack of water, excess of water, physical damage to the stem, ants loosening the soil around the plant, phytophthora a form of 'root rot' that is becoming a considerable menace, etc. Wrongly, if there is wilting the blame is given to stem rot of phoma clematidina.

A rare cause of flopping (wilting) is Flux. This tends to strike thick plant stems as in montanas. The bark splits at one point releasing sap. This may be due to physical damage, frost, or other unproven causes. The sap is sweet, thus organisms, yeasts, fungi, insects quickly move in and a stinking, sticky mess ensues. The damage may not kill the plant. If seen early firmly bandage the stem at the point of damage. It may save the plant. If not, or the damage was not seen at an early stage, then cut through the stem below the damage. Depending on the point of damage the plant will or will not survive. If damage from frost was suspected, protect the tree in subsequent years with horticultural fleece.

PLATE 195.
Flux on two stems of a montana.

The flowers and leaves can be attacked by insects that behave similarly with all plants. However, as the montanas flower earlier than the times when insects are numerous, the montana usually suffers little damage.

Propagation

Montana clematis are no longer propagated commercially by grafting but by soft wood cuttings. The gardener can obtain new plants: 1) by layering, 2) from soft wood and hard wood cuttings, 3) from seeds, 4) by division. Layering is simple and effective:

1.   Layering

This is the best method for producing a small number of montana plants. The advantages are:

a)   The new plant comes true to type with the offspring having the identical characteristics of the parent.

b)   It can extend an existing plant on one or both sides which makes a larger impact. Furthermore, there will be replacement plants should the original plant die.

c)   The layered plant can be used elsewhere in the garden.

Layering can begin as soon as the ground gets warm in early spring. Stems are brought down to ground level and used for the propagation. Layering can be done at any time until the autumn; but in this event the plants may not be ready until the following year. Spring-layered plants will have formed roots by the autumn and will be ready for 'potting up'.

Many of the montanas grow so strongly that it is possible to use a simple method. Just bring a clematis stem down to the ground, make a trench 10–15cm. (4–6in.) deep with your hand or trowel, gently lay the stem in the trench, twist the bark at a node, place the soil over it, place a brick over each node, and fix the end of the stem to a cane. Keep the stem well watered. Using a simple method like this probably means you will attempt to layer more clematis. (See Figure X)

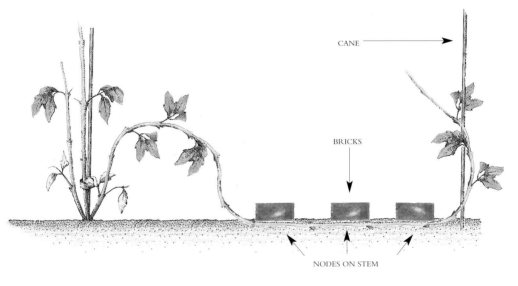

CANE

BRICKS

NODES ON STEM

Figure X.
Simple layering.

A more exact method is as follows:

a)   A long stem is gently brought down towards the ground. Old material, and not green material, is best for layering.

b)   Carefully inspect the stem to see where there are good nodes. With a sharp knife, cut below a node joint, slicing upwards about half-way through the stem to make a short 'tongue'. To keep the 'tongue' open, slip a match or pebble in the elbow. (See Figure XI)

c)   Powder the cut with hormone rooting powder.

d)   With a trowel make a trench 10–15cm. (4–6in.) deep. In the trench place peat and soil or potting compost and soil or sharp sand. Gently peg the node down in this mixture using a piece of wire bent into the shape of a hairpin. Cover the node with the mixture.

e)   Cover the node with a good mulch, a brick, or stones to keep the area moist.

f)   Mark the end of the stem with a short cane to remind you where the layer is and to fix the stem.

g)   Water freely and keep watered.

h)   Leave for six to twelve months. To test whether you have roots, gently pull the end of the stem. If there is resistance you have roots.

i)   With secateurs, sever the layered plant from the parent plant, gently lift with fork and pot up immediately. Do not let the roots dry out. Water the pot. Feed it with liquid fertiliser. When the plant is strong it can be planted out.

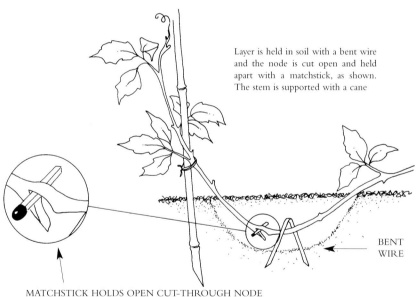

Layer is held in soil with a bent wire and the node is cut open and held apart with a matchstick, as shown. The stem is supported with a cane

BENT WIRE

MATCHSTICK HOLDS OPEN CUT-THROUGH NODE

Figure XI.
Layering a montana.

Serpentine layering

Serpentine layering involves taking a particularly long shoot and a number of nodes. Each of the nodes is treated as above in the ground or in pots in the ground. Part of the stem between nodes is above ground. (See Figure XII)

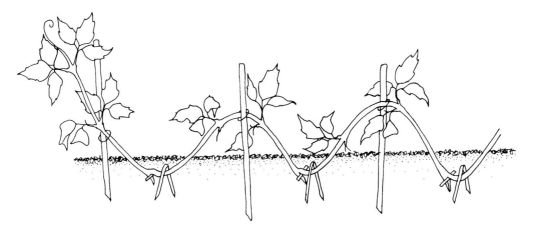

Figure XII.
Serpentine layering.

Instead of putting the node into a trench it can be laid gently into a mixture in a 25cm. (10in.) pot. The mixture can be either soil-based potting compost, peat and soil, or compost and soil. (See Figure XIII)

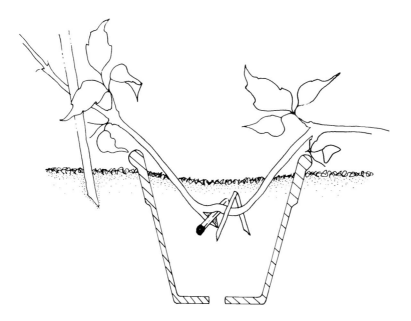

Figure XIII.
Serpentine layering- alternative method.

2.   From Cuttings

Soft wood cuttings. The new plant will of course have the characteristic features of the parent. Proceed as follows:

a)   The sooner the cuttings are taken in the spring the longer time they will have to become good, strong plants before the autumn. Check your plants to see if stems have been produced from which it will be suitable to take cuttings. Cuttings must be taken from stems which are firm and semi-hard. This usually means that the tip of the stem will produce cuttings which are too soft while the bottom part produces those which are too hard. The middle stem, therefore, may be the most suitable and the ideal cutting is one firm enough to slip into the cutting mixture with a firm push.

b)   The potting mixture for the cutting should be half moss peat and half grit (or Perlite). Others advocate two parts sharp sand and one part peat or use soil-based cuttings compost. The mixture should be sterilized.

c)   An inter-nodal cutting is taken (find a node with its leaves, then cut between this node and the one below). Thus there is only a node at the top end of the cutting. The total length of the cutting should be between 2.5–5cm. (1–2in.). (See Figure XIV)

d)   Should you come across a stem with its nodes very close together then you may need to use a nodal cutting. There will be a node at the top and the bottom end of the cutting. (See Figure XV)

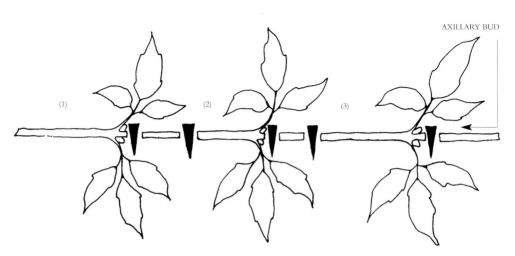

Figure XIV.
Propagation from cuttings.

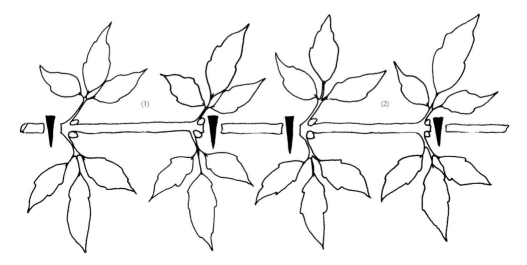

Figure XV.
Propagation from cuttings.

e)   Spread the clematis stem on a bench and make the cuttings with a
       sharp knife or razor blade. Keep the cuttings moist and use at once.
f)   Trim off completely one set of the pair of leaves. The leaf that
       remains can also have its central leaflet cut off. (See Figure XVI)

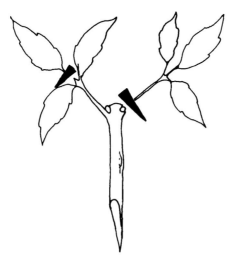

Figure XVI.
Propagation from cuttings.

g)   Quickly dip the cutting in water and then into hormone rooting powder, allowing a dip of about 2.5cm. (1in.) of the stem.

h)   Gently but firmly push the cutting into the compost of the pot until the buds are resting on its surface. Avoid the cuttings coming into contact with one another. The cuttings should be 8cm (3in) apart with the leaves not touching each other, the compost or the pot's cover. Label the pot.

i)   Spray the pot with water containing a fungicide. Let the pot drain for at least 24 hours. The type of fungicide used should be changed every ten days.

j)   Put the pot into either a propagator, a cold frame, or a pot covered with polythene. In the latter event, place four stakes at the circumference of the pot, to keep the polythene away from the leaves. (See Figure XVII) The plants must be kept in the shade. If bottom heating is available, it can be helpful in producing rooting. The temperature should be about 23°C (73°F). Continue spraying with fungicide once a week, i.e. the container taken out of its cover, sprayed, allowed to drain, and then put back again.

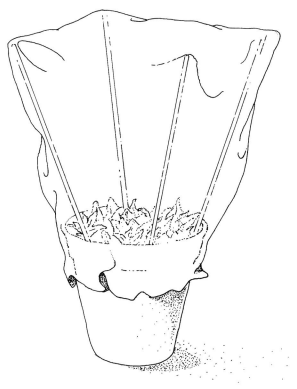

Figure XVII.
A simple propagator made from a pot covered with polythene over a framework of sticks, as shown.

k)   The cuttings will root in about four to five weeks and it is usually obvious which have been successful. Tug gently on the cutting and if there is resistance roots have formed.

l)   A little air can now be allowed to the plants and increased each day until, in a few days, the cover is taken off.

m)   After a further two to three weeks, plant out into 10cm (4in) pots, using a suitable potting mixture. Pinch or nip out any central growth to encourage side shoots. Continue to spray with fungicide every week.

n)   If good growth is made, the plants can be planted in the next largest pot. Again, pinch out the central growth to encourage side growth. Keep spraying with fungicide once a week. Give liquid fertiliser once a week.

o)   The plants can be planted out in the following spring or can be kept for a further year in a pot. By now you are admiring the hard work of a nurseryman!

Hard Wood Cuttings

This method applies particularly to strong growing clematis such as the montanas. The hardwood cuttings should be taken in early spring or even late winter.

The end of an inter-nodal cutting should be bruised or wounded by taking a sliver off the bottom. Some use double nodal cuttings. The cutting should be about 10cm. (4in.) long. The cuttings are placed, 10cm. (4in.) apart in a trench in the garden. If successful the cuttings can be 'potted up' late in the year into 10cm. (4in.) pots. These are kept in a protected area until the spring and will do well if the pots are sunk into a trench in a sheltered area of the garden.

Some claim success with the cuttings in a pot containing a mixture of 50% peat and 50% grit. Pots are kept in a cold greenhouse.

3.   Seeds

The seed or achene of the clematis consists of a base containing the seed and a tail of silky hairs which helps dispersal by the wind. The new plant will resemble the parent plant but may be poorer although a few may be better.

Select the seed from good plants. The seeds from the montanas may be ready by midsummer and can be used then. If they are stored they should be kept in a cotton bag, labelled and put into a refrigerator where they can be chilled below 40°F (4°C) but not frozen.

The seed will germinate in a seed medium in seed pans. Prick out as soon as the seedlings can be handled and put into a soil based compost. Seeds of the montanas will usually germinate quickly and produce seedlings in one season. Seedlings are potted up into small pots, 'potted on' to larger ones, and in two to three years may produce a bloom.

Chance Seedlings

When hoeing keep an eye out for the chance seedlings of montanas. The seedlings may have come from a nearby plant or from a cross between two of your montanas in the garden. Most of the seedlings will be worthless even though unique. To be worthwhile a new plant must display the characteristics not yet available in an existing plant. However, some well-known montanas have come about in this way such as *C. montana* 'Freda'.

4.   Division of a montana

This should be undertaken in spring, immediately after flowering. It should only be employed with montanas that make small plants. The stems are pruned nearly to the ground. The whole plant is carefully lifted and divided into two or more pieces. The division should be done with a sharp knife, spade, or fork. (See Figure XVIII) The pieces of plant are put straight back into the ground prepared for clematis or if they are small, planted in pots and later, when they are large enough, planted outside. Keep the pieces watered.

Figure XVIII.
Division of a montana using the two fork method.

Hybridising

As amateur gardeners have more spare time than the nurseries, some turn their hand to hybridising and can be very successful at it. Here an entirely new plant is produced by crossing one plant with another. For those who have the knowledge and the time this is the most exciting aspect of clematis culture. It produces something unique and valuable. The principles are the same as for hybridising in any genus and any interested reader should consult the specialist literature.

Hardiness Ratings

USA

In the USA a convenient zonal system for plant hardiness has been developed by the United States Department of Agriculture (USDA). This divides the country into eleven zones depending on the annual minimum temperature for each zone. See Table I which gives the average minimum temperature for each zone.

At Table II will be found the zones appropriate for optimum growth in each clematis Group. The lowest number indicates the zone with the lowest temperature for survival. Clematis will not usually thrive in Zones 1 and 2, without special care. The highest number indicates the zone with the highest temperature for reliable growth; this is usually Zone 9 for clematis. Clematis can adapt to Zones 10 and 11, given suitable micro-climates.

An American gardener will usually know the zone on the USDA classification to which his garden belongs. The American gardener can see from Table II that the montanas belong to Group IV and can be grown in Zones 7, 8 and 9. This means that the winter temperature of his garden should be above −18°C. (0°F). With a favourable micro-climate and with special care (see p.161) he may be able to grow at a lower winter temperature than this. If the gardener lives in a zone with a higher winter temperature than −1°C (30°F) (Zones 10 and 11) the summer temperature may be too high for growing montanas without special care. Again it may be possible to adjust the microclimate (see p.162) and make success possible.

World-wide

From the Tables I and II it is also possible to establish world-wide ratings. Knowing the annual minimum temperature for your area in the world you can find your zone in Table I. For example, consulting Table I, an annual minimum temperature for your area below −40°C puts you in Zone 2. Consulting Table II you can see that it makes it difficult for you to grow any group of clematis. Consulting Table I again, a minimum annual temperature of −9°C puts you in Zone 8 and you can grow all groups of clematis, whereas a minimum annual temperature of 5°C puts you in Zone 11 and it will be too hot for most clematis to thrive in your garden without special care, or a favourable micro-climate.

A Reminder

A gardener must always take account of the micro-climate in his garden which may differ from the zone rating for that area because of elevation, closeness to the sea or lakes, prevailing winds, rainfall, humidity, frost pockets, etc. Thus a gardener, because of his micro-climate or adjustment to it, may be able to grow montanas in a zone not usually thought suitable for growing these plants.

TABLE I

Zone	Fahrenheit	Celsius
Zone 1	below −50°	below− 45°
Zone 2	−50° to −40°	− 5° to −40°
Zone 3	−40° to −30°	−40° to −34°
Zone 4	−30° to −20°	−34° to −29°
Zone 5	− 0° to −10°	−29° to −23°
Zone 6	−10° to − 0°	−23° to −18°
Zone 7	0° to 10°	−18° to −12°
Zone 8	10° to 20°	−12° to − 7°
Zone 9	20° to 30°	− 7° to 1°
Zone 10	30° to 40°	− 1° to 4°
Zone 11	Above 40°	Above 4°

TABLE II

		USA	World-Wide (Minimum Winter Temp.)
Group I	Evergreen	Zone 6–9	Above −23°C
Group II	Alpina	Zone 3–9	Above −40°C
Group III	Macropetala	Zone 3–9	Above −40°C
Group IV	Montana	Zone 7–9	Above −18°C
Group V	Rockery	Zone 7–9	Above − 8°C
Group VI	Early Large Flowered	Zone 4–9	Above −34°C
Group VII	Late Large Flowered	Zone 3–9	Above −40°C
Group VIII	Herbaceous	Zone 3–9	Above −40°C
Group IX	Viticella	Zone 3–9	Above − 0°C
Group X	Texensis	Zone 4–9	Above −34°C
Group XI	Orientalis	Zone 4–9	Above − 4°C
Group XII	Late	Zone 3–9	Above −40°C

Round the Year Care of Montana Clematis

Mid-winter
Order tools, peat, manure, fertilisers, chemicals, etc.
Water any plants liable to dry out.
Establish, or bring up to date, a plan showing location of the montana clematis.

Late Winter
Water plants liable to dry out.
Order clematis catalogues.
Plan new plantings of montanas.
Prepare clematis beds to be planted in early spring. Dig holes in preparation for planting later.
Check name labels on all montanas.
Move small montanas if required.
Divide small montana plants if desired.
Take hard wood cuttings.

Early Spring
Plant montanas if conditions allow.
Weed beds.
Take hard wood cuttings.

Mid-Spring
Apply general fertiliser to the montanas.
Start watering programme.

Late Spring
Apply mulch of manure or other suitable material to the clematis.
Layer montana stems.
Continue watering programme.
Take soft wood cuttings.

Early Summer
Apply second feeding of fertiliser.
Continue watering programme.
Collect montana seed for sowing.

Mid-Summer
Continue watering programme.

Late Summer
Continue watering programme.

Early Autumn
Prepare clematis beds if planting in autumn is desired.
Reduce watering when possible.

Mid–Autumn
Tidy beds.
Plant montanas if autumn planting is desired.
Reduce watering programme.

Late Autumn
Protect clematis in cold areas.

Early Winter
Water any plants liable to dry out.

Hemisphere Differences

In order to make the text useful in both hemispheres, plant flowering times, etc, are described in terms of seasons, not months. The following table translates seasons into months for the two hemispheres.

TABLE III

Northern Hemisphere		Southern Hemisphere
Mid-winter	January	Mid-summer
Late winter	February	Late summer
Early spring	March	Early autumn
Mid-spring	April	Mid-autumn
Late spring	May	Late autumn
Early summer	June	Early winter
Mid-summer	July	Mid-winter
Late summer	August	Late winter
Early autumn	September	Early spring
Mid-autumn	October	Mid-spring
Late autumn	November	Late spring
Early winter	December	Early summer

Chapter VI
Displaying Your Montanas

There is no garden, however small, that cannot benefit from planting at least one montana. Early in the year when there is so little to catch the eye, it raises the spirits to have a sudden sweep of colour and heralds the joys to come in the garden.

Some Principles of Display

1. Flowering Time

The montanas flower in mid-spring through late spring to early summer. In warm areas they will be earlier in the year, in cold areas they will be later in the year. Flowering in early season has the advantage of producing dramatic colour when gardens lack colour. It has the disadvantage that flowering can be adversely affected, in a bad year, by frost.

If matching of the flowers of the montanas is desired, it must be with shrubs, climbers, and roses flowering at that time of the year, e.g. wisteria, honeysuckle, lilac, laburnum, ceonathus, *solanum crispa*, actinidia and early climbing roses such as 'Meg', 'Gloire de Dijon', 'Maigold', 'Zephirine Drouhin', 'Albertine'.

PLATE 196.
C.montana flowering with lilac.

2. Flowering period

This is short – usually about three weeks. This handicap is outweighed by the massive impact of the montanas even though the period be short. The period can be considerably extended by having a sequence of flowering montanas, e.g. 1) *C.gracilifolia*, 2) 'Elizabeth', 3) 'Rubens', 4) 'Mayleen', 5) 'White Fragrance', 6) *C. chrysocoma*, 7) 'Continuity', 8) *C.* 'Wilsonii'. This sequence can extend over three months.

3. Size

Some of the montanas are enormous. They can overwhelm a shrub, a rose, a tree, and even a whole garden. I am reminded of the photograph of Mr Jones of Menai Bridge, North Wales, U.K., whose garden and some of his neighbours', consisted of just one plant, 'Mayleen'! Mr Jones was hard pressed to find anywhere to show himself to the camera. The photograph seemed to have been taken from a helicopter!

The size is, of course, an advantage for dramatic colour but the plant must be positioned where it cannot do damage to other plants. Also select the montana appropriate to the size of the area you have chosen for it.

Some large montanas are *C. montana*, 'East Malling', 'Elizabeth', 'Grandiflora', 'Mayleen', 'Pink Perfection', 'Rubens' and 'White Fragrance'.

Medium sized montanas are 'Alexander', 'Broughton Star', *C. chrysocoma*, 'Continuity', 'Fragrant Spring', 'Gothenburg', 'Jacqui', 'Lilacina', 'Marjorie', 'New Dawn', 'Odorata', 'Olga', 'Vera', 'Warwickshire Rose' and 'Rosea'. Given very favourable growing conditions these can emulate the large montanas.

Small sized montanas are 'Freda', 'Margaret Jones', 'New Dawn', 'Pleniflora', 'Picton's Variety', 'Tetrarose' and 'Veitch'.

Allow room for a montana to reach its optimum size without encroaching on another montana. Thus montanas must be planted at least 1.8m. (6ft.) apart.

4. Colour

The colour of the montanas is predominantly white, pale pink, pink, and dark pink. These are colours that brighten shady areas and stand out against dark foliage – in fact any foliage.

The darker the pink in the flower as in 'Freda', 'Warwickshire Rose', the darker the montana foliage.

The dark foliage of montanas can be an excellent background to other flowers, shrubs and climbers throughout the year, until winter.

Red and white flowers are colour-harmonious to pink montanas. Blue flowers on the other hand are contrasting to pink montanas. (See Plate 197.)

Colour of walls should be taken into account. Brick walls should be avoided, if possible, as montanas are mostly a shade of pink and they look best against white walls.

PLATE 197.
'Tetrarose' makes a fine contrast to blue wisteria.

PLATE 198.
Spring colour.

5. The habit of the plant

This changes through the year and is in three stages. 1) in spring there is a dramatic burst of colour (see Plate 198); 2) for the rest of the year there is foliage, often attractive (see Plate 199); 3) in winter there are no leaves, thus the effect can be drab (see Plate 200).

PLATE 199.
Summer foliage.

PLATE 200.
Winter twigs.

The above argues for not planting montanas where they are conspicuous in winter. The ideal way of reducing their drab impact then is to plant them with evergreen shrubs and trees, and up trees, even deciduous trees. You 'tuck them away' as much as you can. After flowering the mass of montana foliage is excellent background for other shrubs, climbers and plants.

6. Scent

Some of the montanas have the most powerful and attractive fragrance of all scented plants, e.g. 'Elizabeth', 'Fragrant Spring', 'Mayleen', 'Odorata', 'Rubens' and 'White Fragrance'. It is useful to bring this perfume to garden visitors by planting close to arches, gates, seats, and pathways.

PLATE 201.
The fragrance of 'Mayleen' almost overwhelms anyone passing through this gate.

7. Planting with host plants

If it is desired to plant the montanas with host shrubs, climbers, and plants, then this can be done in five ways:

i).   Use the host as a background to the montana, e.g. montana into an evergreen shrub or tree.   (See Plate 202)

ii).   Try to match the colour of the montana with the colour of the host, e.g. a montana and the leaves of actinidia. (See Plate 203)

iii).   Use the host after it has flowered as a background for a flowering montana, e.g. a montana flowering into the attractive foliage of a prunus. (See Plate 204)

PLATE 202.
A montana shows up well against a conifer.

PLATE 203.
A montana and the foliage of actinidia.

PLATE 204.
A montana into a prunus after it flowered.

PLATE 205.
'Grandiflora' with rose 'Compassion'.

iv).   Use the montana low down on a larger plant, e.g. a short montana on the lower branches of the rose 'Wedding Day'.

v).   The montana can be planted near a host plant with an overlap that endangers neither plant but allows a fine harmonious colour effect, e.g. Clematis 'Grandiflora' and rose 'Compassion'. (See Plate 205.)

8. Protection

Bear in mind the need of some tender montanas for winter protection. A house wall out of the wind may allow survival when an open position would not, e.g. for tender montanas such as 'Picton's Variety', *C. chrysocoma*, 'Continuity' and 'Rosea'. Sometimes a protective location may lead to semi-shade. This will usually be tolerated with the bonus that the flowers will not fade quickly.

9. Multiple planting

With smaller clematis it is possible to plant more than one clematis on a support structure or host plant. This is rarely possible with the montanas because of the area they cover. Exceptions would be long walls, long pergolas or a very large arbour.

10. Permanent structure

A montana plant is a permanent structure in the landscape of the garden. It cannot be severely pruned as you can with other groups. Thus it is always there. Furthermore it is there for many years.

Physical Supports for Montanas

Wood

A simple way of giving support is by the use of posts or poles which can be used at points in the garden where there is no natural support. Poles can give height to a display of montanas in a herbaceous border. Again the post with a montana can be a special feature on a lawn.

   Posts should be of hard wood. They must be buried deep enough into the ground so that they can withstand not only the weight of the clematis but also the stress of the wind. A 3.5m. (12ft.) post with 1m. (3ft.) of the post in the ground meets the purpose. It is possible to use a metal spike, which is sunk into the ground or concrete. (See Figure XIX.) The post can also fit into a metal plate; the post fitting into this has a longer life, is easier to replace and does not move when under stress. (See Figure XX.) The posts can also be fixed into concrete. Some experienced experts however maintain that it is not wind stress that hurts posts but the water collecting round them that rots them. This argues for ramming soil hard against a deeply positioned post.

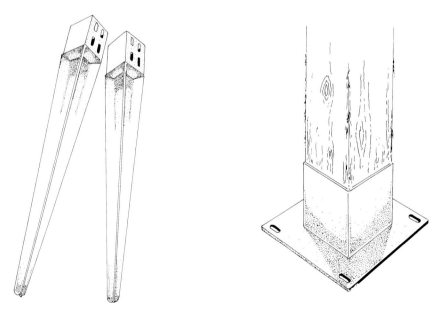

Figure XIX.   **Figure XX.**

The montana needs to be tied to the pole and to make this possible the pole should be surrounded by wire netting or wire running vertically.

Much ingenuity can be employed over the use of posts. A single post or a row of posts can be placed along the length of a border, along the side of a path, at intervals in a shrubbery, or as a partition between one part of the garden and another. Three posts can be brought together to form a pyramid or tripod on which the clematis climbs. Another interesting way of employing posts is to have an umbrella at the top (such as an inverted hanging basket). (Figure XXI)

Yet another attractive method of display is to run a rope, a chain or a wire between two posts; the montana is encouraged to run along the support between the two posts thus giving the effect of festooning. (Figure XXII)

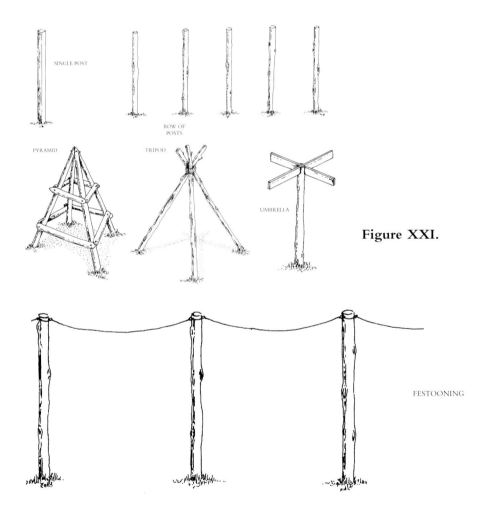

Figure XXI.

Figure XXII.

PLATE 206.
Hill House montana support.

Two posts together with a third pole above make an arch. The arch should be 2–2.5m. (7-8ft.) tall to allow comfortable access. Arches can also make an arbour, bower, gazebo or rotunda. Posts can also be used to make a pergola. It can be of simple rustic posts or hardwood. The wooden supports discussed here are most suitable for small and medium-sized montanas. A long pergola or fence can support a number of smaller or medium-sized montanas. The same principles apply to clematis on wooden fences, trellises or screens. There are many types of fences – close boarded, paling, post and rail, post and wire, chain link, interwoven panels. A trellis should be supported on walls by battens.

Hill House Montana Support

This was developed as I had run out of trees as montana supports. Construction is easy. A 3.5m. (12ft.) post, rot proof, is purchased from wood suppliers. The same source will supply 3m. (9ft.) roof slats. The slats are cut into 1m. (3ft.) lengths. These are nailed at intervals to the upper 3m. (9ft.), i.e. the portion above ground. A 1m. (3ft.) hole is dug with a special heavy spade which, if employed, digs the hole very quickly. 1m. (3ft.) of the post goes into the hole. (See Plate 206)

In one season the post will be largely covered by the montana, making an attractive mound of plant that blends beautifully with the rest of the garden. I had feared that I would spend the summer tying in the clematis shoots. I feared in vain. Once a shoot reaches the next level of the support the rest of the shoots follow – until they reach the top of the pole. The montana does it all! (See Plate 207)

Metal

Metal supports can match all the uses of the wood supports. Single metal structures take the place of a pole or pillar. Combinations of single structures make arches, arbours, pergolas, bowers, gazebos and fences, including chain link fences. (Figure XXIII).

PLATE 207.
'Odorata' makes a fine show on a Hill House montana support.

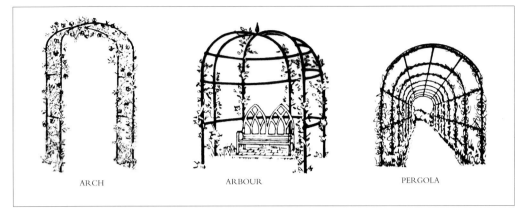

ARCH   ARBOUR   PERGOLA

Figure XXIII.

Stone and Brick

Stone structures can match most of the uses of the wooden structures. We can use stone and bricks to make pillars, arches, porches, bowers, pergolas, gazebos, colonnades and gateways. (See Plate 208)

PLATE 208.
A montana covers the gateway to 'Sea View', home of the poet Dylan Thomas in his blissful early marriage.

Walls

Walls can be those of a house, a garage or an outbuilding. Walls can surround a garden or divide it. Short montanas look particularly effective on short walls running alongside steps or climbing over balustrades. The montanas can surround windows or grace porches. (Plate 209)

A montana can be alone on a wall but this is not ideal as in winter all that can be seen are almost barren stalks. It is more effective to plant the montana between other climbing plants.

When planting on a wall, a number of points must be borne in mind. The montana, as was discussed earlier, must be planted well away from the wall – at least 60cm. (2ft.) – and led back by string, wire or cane. The perspective is enhanced if the spread of the clematis is roughly equivalent to its height. Should the clematis prove too high for the wall, the upper tresses can be led down again towards the ground by wire, string or cane, giving a waterfall effect. Low-growing clematis can be planted to hide any bare legs of montanas.

PLATE 209.
'Grandiflora' covers the main walls of a cottage, 'Elizabeth' covers the far corner, while 'Vera', 'Gothenberg'and 'Rubens' cover the garden wall.

Roofs

The roof of a shed is one of the most difficult areas to beautify. Wire it in horizontal lengths and the clematis are encouraged to grow along them, tied in, giving sensational results (Plate 210). 'Continuity' is particularly effective.

Figures

Any figures you have in the garden can be brought into your decorative scheme (See Plate 211).

PLATE 210.
'Continuity' covers a shed roof.

PLATE 211.
'Tetrarose' beautifies a little girl.

Training Montanas

It is necessary to have strong horizontal wire supports to hold montanas on walls. The simplest support is a wire running between two nails. It is much better to use galvanised nails, or better still, masonry nails on which there is a clip that the wire can run through. A stronger support comes from using vine eyes driven into the walls at intervals and through which the wire can run (Figure XXIV), but the strongest support of all is given by screw eyes. A hole is drilled in the wall where a rawlplug is inserted and into which a screw is turned (Figure XXV). The wire should be of a gauge strong enough to withstand the weight of the clematis, and the force of the wind. It should be secured at 1.2m. (4ft.) intervals and be 45cm. (1½ft.) apart. The wire should be 5cm. (2in.) away from the wall as this allows the stem of the montana to reach behind the wire and cling to it, thus when it is necessary to repair or redecorate the wall the clematis will fall away easily in one piece and lie tidily on the ground.

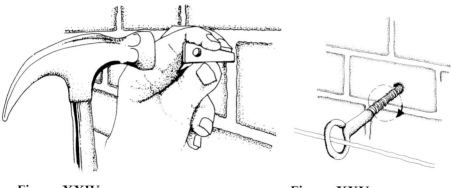

Figure XXIV.   **Figure XXV.**

Tying in Montanas

The montana is tied directly to the support or, uncommonly, to a host plant already on the support. A number of ties can be used. Raffia can be used where the tie does not need to be permanent, though green string is preferable and unobtrusive. Plastic coated wire is permanent and quick to use. It should not be allowed to squeeze the stem too tightly and room must be allowed for growth in the diameter of the stem. The gardener soon becomes adept at using these plastic ties.

Natural Support for Montanas

Montanas look their best with other large plants. The effect can be stunning.

With Trees

Montanas being large plants can climb into a large tree. The smaller montanas fit admirably into small trees. Some points need to be borne in mind in growing clematis into trees. The tree should be well established before the montana grows into it; the weight of a montana in a strong wind is considerable which the tree must be robust enough to bear. The montana should never be so vigorous as to suffocate the tree, or vice versa; the two must be matched. The clematis should be allowed to grow as naturally as possible in the tree. However, quite often, judicious tying in of the clematis can help the final shape and also reduces the weight on them during winter storms. For very large montanas try a large mature Scots Pine. A large holly tree is fine background for a medium sized montana.

The aim is to show the montana off to advantage and bring interest and colour to a tree which is not blooming and would otherwise be dull and uninteresting. Not only must account be taken of the colour of the clematis but also of the colour and form of the tree foliage. In general, the white and pink montanas do best against dark trees and the brighter pink plants against the lighter ones.

Evergreen Trees

An evergreen tree particularly benefits from a combination with a montana as, of course, it rarely develops flowers. (See Plate 212)

PLATE 212.
A montana climbs high into an enormous holly tree.

Deciduous Trees

Somewhere, sometime, almost every tree has been host to a montana – with spectacular results (See Plate 213).

PLATE 213.
A montana grows into a laburnum tree.

Planting Near a Tree

It must be remembered that the soil and conditions around a tree are not very kind to a clematis; the soil is often dry and has been exhausted by the tree and may also be shaded. All these deficiencies have to be countered.

It is usual to advise that clematis should be planted on the shady side of the tree so that the light at the other side of the tree will pull the clematis through it. Furthermore, it is assumed that the clematis will benefit from any moisture in the shade. Unhappily the shade is often of such depth that the clematis refuses to take off. So it is often better to plant on the sunny side of the tree and lead the clematis into it by canes or string; once the clematis has reached the tree, it will then take its own course.

A heavy mulching is necessary to compensate for the sun drying the ground. How close the montana is planted depends on the shape of the tree. An upright tree has roots that go straight into the ground and the branches offer little shade close to the tree. In this case the montana can be planted within 1m. (3ft.) of the tree trunk (Figure XXVI). A globe-shaped tree has deep shade around its trunk. Here the montana must be planted at the edge of the tree out of the shade. This may be 2–2½m. (6–8ft.) from the trunk, and led into the branches above it (Figure XXVII). In this way the montana will have sun and good soil for initial growth and the rain will reach them.

Figure XXVI.

Figure XXVII.

Even when the clematis stems are woody and strong, a cane should always be kept alongside the stem. Then it is less easy for someone to blunder against the stem and break it (games on the lawn can bring damage).

The size of a tree will determine the number of montanas that can climb into it – usually only one. Unusually, consider multiple planting for dramatic effect: two or three of the same montana can be used, or two or three different varieties flowering in sequence will give colour over a longer period.

With Shrubs

The general principles are as for trees. The montana must be of small size. The shrub should be allowed to reach its optimum size and height before clematis is carried into it when it must also be able to withstand the weight of the clematis (See Plate 214). A too vigorous montana can kill a shrub while too weak a montana can be killed by its host. The shrub and the clematis must also be matched for flower colour and foliage. Shrubs of dark foliage will match best with light and pink montanas. Shrubs with light foliage on the other hand are more suitable for strong pink and red montanas.

Some of the best results, and safest, are when a part only of a montana is allowed to creep into a shrub such as a lilac. A careful watch is undertaken to prevent the montana overpowering the shrub.

PLATE 214.
A medley of montanas sport amongst rhododendrons.

Planting Near a Shrub

The clematis must be planted at least 60cm. (2ft.) away from the edge of the shrub and led to it on a cane, string or wire. Wire can be pegged near the clematis and the wire or green string carried over the shrub to the other side in the direction in which you want the montana to grow. It should be planted on the sunny side to encourage growth, and given a good mulching to retain moisture in the sun. The point of exit of the clematis from the soil must be marked with a cane, otherwise it is likely to be hoed up when you work on the shrubbery. Careful attention must be given to watering.

In Borders

Montanas can be used to give height to a border by growing them on a support such as a post, a tripod, an umbrella or Hill House montana supports (see Plate 215.). Make sure the montanas are sufficiently apart so as not to climb into one another.

PLATE 215.
'Olga' and 'Unity' add beauty to a border.

As Creeping or Ground Cover Plants

Given large barren ground areas some gardeners have found a valuable use for even the largest montanas. In the right place in the spring the result can be spectacular.

With Climbing roses

Climbing roses are a fine companion to clematis. However, great care has to be employed that the montanas do not swamp the roses.

Methods that can be employed include:

1. Allowing the edges of the montana area to ease into a climbing rose. As the montanas flower early, the match will be with early flowering roses such as yellow 'Gloire de Dijon' and 'Maigold' and pink 'Albetine', 'Meg', 'Madame Grégoire Staechelin' and 'Compassion' (See Plate 216).

2. The small montanas e.g. 'Freda', 'Picton's Variety', 'Veitch' can, with care, grow into a well developed climbing rose such as white 'Iceberg' and white 'New Dawn', yellow 'Casino', pink 'Compassion', red 'Galway Bay', pink 'Pink Perpétue' and pink 'Summer Wine', and red 'Park Direktor Riggers'.
    The montana is not pruned so the plant will remain with the rose throughout the year. One year the montana will flower before the rose, another year with the rose, and yet another year, after the rose.

3. A small montana can grace the lower regions of massive climbing roses such as 'Wedding Day' and Filipes 'Kiftsgate'.

PLATE 216.
'Elizabeth' creeps into rose 'Compassion' and gives point to its flowers.

With Shrub roses

With care the small montanas can be grown with well-developed shrub roses such as yellow 'Canary Bird' and 'Frühlingsgold', pink 'Ballerina' and white 'Nevada'.

With other climbing plants

With care, always bearing in mind their vigour, montanas can be grown into other vigorous climbing plants. (See Plate 217) With good fortune the montana may even flower at the same time as a early flowering host, e.g. wisteria.

With other clematis

Other groups of clematis may be flowering at the same time as the montanas. (See Plate 218) These will be late growing alpinas and macropetalas, and early growing large flowered clematis. The latter will include 'Lasurstern', 'Nelly Moser', 'Guernsey Cream', 'H.F. Young'. A lovely combination can be made of these climbing into the edge of a large white or pink montana.

PLATE 217.
'Rubens' slides into *Solanum crispum*.

PLATE 218.
The blue 'H.F. Young' is a companion to the pink 'Mayleen'.

Patio

If there is a choice between making a hole in the patio for a montana or planting in a container, choose the hole. All clematis will flourish in the ground beneath the patio as the stonework makes an ideal mulch. Water the hole, go away happily for the weekend. Return. Water again. Go away for a week. Furthermore the montana will grow strongly in Mother Earth. The face of the hole can be beautified with stones, etc., but leave a small channel for the water to percolate from the rain falling on the patio. All the montanas can be used for planting in the patio hole, depending on the requirements of the site.

Containers

If it is not possible to plant directly into the ground then containers will have to be employed. Even the smallest montana is a large and vigorous plant thus they will need a large container – even to the size of a half-barrel. Stone is the best material but it can be very heavy. Wood is satisfactory but plastic least so.

As important as regular watering is drainage. This can come from stones in the bottom, ample drainage holes, and lifting the container off the ground. Compost must be rich; if in doubt use John Innes No 3. The copious watering the plant will receive will leach away the minerals in your compost, so supplement with liquid fertiliser. Every two years boldly take away about a third of the compost, starting at the edge and moving in; replace with good compost.

In cold areas your plant may need protection with horticultural fleece or sacking. Reduce watering in winter but do not let the container dry out.

If the montana is not too large and detachable, the container and plant may be moved to a protected site or even indoors. Platforms with wheels are available for moving containers.

It might be thought that containers should only contain the small montanas but even the largest, such as 'Grandiflora' and 'Mayleen' do well. They will, however, be conveniently much reduced in size because they are growing in a restricted root area. (See Plate 219)

PLATE 219.
Giant 'Mayleen' has been restricted by being grown in a wooden barrel at the bottom right of the picture.

Using montana foliage

After flowering the montanas make large areas of foliage ranging from light green to almost black foliage e.g. 'Warwickshire Rose'. These areas of foliage can be used as a background for other climbing plants e.g. annual climbing plants. Furthermore, yet to flower in the garden are six more strong clematis groups. They can flower on montana foliage as a background.

These are:
Group 7) the Late Large Flowered,
Group 8) the Herbaceous,
Group 9) the Viticellas,
Group 10) the Texenis,
Group 11) the Orientalis,
Group 12) the Autumn Group.

   They can all be pruned off the montana foliage after flowering. 'Mayleen' is in full flower on a wall (Plate 220). It finishes flowering and 'Perle d'Azur' climbs into it using its foliage as a background. The imposter will be pruned to the ground after flowering leaving the 'Mayleen' foliage ready for its spring display. (Plate 221)

PLATE 220.
'Mayleen' in full flower on a wall.

PLATE 221.
'Perle d'Azur' on 'Mayleen' foliage.

Chapter VII
Historical Notes

Clematis montana var. *wilsonii*

E. H. Wilson (1876–1930) undertook four expeditions to China. The first two (starting 1899 and 1903) were for the firm of Veitch and Sons of Chelsea, England. The last two (starting 1906 and 1910) were sponsored by the Arnold Arboretum, Boston, U.S.A.

He first found *C. montana* var. *wilsonii* in October, 1904, on the second Veitch expedition, and again on the first Arnold Arboretum expedition. It is said that it had already been collected by Dr Augustine Henry (1857–1930) before 1900 (No. 10748 of his herbarium specimens). The plant was introduced by Veitch as *C. repens.*

C. montana var. *wilsonii* was described in *Bot. Magazine*, Vol.137. in 1910. TAB.8365, as follows:

'Shrub, climbing; stems striate puberulous. Leaves opposite, 3-foliolate; petioles 1½–4in. long, finely sparingly puberulous; stalks of the end leaflet ⅔–1in. long, twice or thrice as long as those of the lateral leaflets; leaflets ovate narrowly acuminate, truncate or subcordate, those of the flowering shoots elliptic and narrowed to the base, 1½–3in. long, 1–⅕in. wide, wide serrate with apiculate teeth; thin, glabrous above, puberulous on the nerves beneath; nerves sunk above, raised beneath. Flowers fascicled on short leafy branchlets clothed with bud-scales at the base. Peduncles 1-flowered, slender, 6–8in. long, puberulous. Sepals 4, petaloid, white, induplicate-valvate, obovate-oblong, retuse but mucronulate at the tip, ¾–1in. long, about ½in. wide, glabrous within, almost so along a central band outside, but densely pubescent elsewhere. Petals 0. Stamens many, the outer ⅜in long, the inner under ½in. long; filaments linear, glabrous; anthers linear or narrow oblong, 1–1⅕in. long; dehiscence lateral. Carpels many; ovary compressed, glabrous; style glabrous above, silky hairy elsewhere.'

The description was accompanied by a figure made of a plant flowering at the Veitch Nursery in July 1909. That is reproduced here. The conspicuous stamens, mucronate (tipped) large tepals and veined leaves are readily seen (Figure XXVIII). Enlarged figures of a stamen and a carpel are also reproduced.

Wilson referred to the plant in his *Aristocrats of the Garden* as a 'desirable plant'. He also refers to the 'var. wilsonii' plant in his *More Aristocrats of the Garden*, 1928, and included a photograph (reproduced on the right). The large flower, prominent stamens, mucronate (tipped), retused (notched) tepals and veined leaves are easily observed.

The plant was thought to be lost. However, in 1986 in the International Clematis Society's Newsletter, Mr Lawrence Banks of Hergest Croft, Kington, U.K. in an article headed '*Clematis montana* var. *wilsonii*' announced he had found a plant in his garden. He conjectured it had been planted in the garden before the 1914–18 war. He compared his plant with descriptions

Figure XXVIII.

PLATE 222.
Wilson's 'desirable' plant.

in the Veitch catalogue of the period, the description in the *Botanical Magazine* (t8365) and that in the second edition of Bean. He stated that his plant exactly matched those descriptions. In *The Clematis*, 1997 he reminded clematarians of the plant and pressed them 'to inspect this remarkable survivor'. The plant is enormous and spreads itself over a large gate and neighbouring shrubs. No doubt to distinguish this plant from the other so-called 'Wilsonii' (now 'White Fragrance') it became usual to refer to Banks' plant as 'Hergest Form'. This addition is no longer required as the other plant is not a 'Wilsonii'.

More good fortune occurred. In his book *Clematis*, 1989, Mr Barry Fretwell described a plant from seed collected in China which he suspected 'must be close to the old wilsonii'. He describes it as follows:

'The flowers are large for a montana, 3in. (8cm.) across, the four sepals obovate, wide across the blunt tips but gappy. The colour is pure white, and one of its most striking features is one not found in the old *C. wilsonii*, namely a boss of the longest stamens I have seen in any clematis. The long, thread-like filaments, with yellow stamens, shimmer as strongly as in any hypericum or eucryphia. Unfortunately it does not possess any scent, while *C. wilsonii* was described as strongly scented. The flowers are borne on the old wood, as in other montanas; by the time the display begins, the plant is a mass of new growth, although the blooms are not obscured by the foliage as they are borne on 12–15 in. (30–38cm.) long flower stalks.

'As befits a montana so different from the rest of its kin, the foliage, too, is markedly distinctive. Although the ternate leaves are serrated, they are more blunt, giving a soft, rounded outline. The area between the veins is raised, creating a textured, quilted effect, with sparse silver hair. Although the plant is sturdy enough it is far less vigorous than the type plant.'

PLATE 223.
'Peveril' on the left and *wilsonii* 'Hergest' on the right.

PLATE 224.
Leaf of *C. wilsonii* 'Hergest' on the left and leaf of 'Peveril' on the right.

PLATE 225.
'White Fragrance'.

Mr. Fretwell was concerned that his plants had two features not seen in the other *C. wilsonii* – no scent and a boss of long stamens. He may have been thinking of the other Wilsonii (now named 'White Fragrance'), which has strong scent but not conspicuous stamens. The plant described above from the *Botanical Magazine*, like his plant, has no scent but has conspicuous stamens. Mr. Fretwell could not call his plant 'Wilsonii' as it seemed to lack two essential features – no scent and long stamens. So he named it 'Peveril'. However, the photograph of his plant, named 'Perveril' by Mr. Fretwell, (Fretwell, Barry. *Clematis*. 1988, p.123) is remarkably like the figure of *C. wilsonii* from the *Botanical Magazine* and the photograph of *C. montana* var. *wilsonii* in *More Aristocrates of the Garden*, all have the retused (notched) and mucronate (pointed) tepals, numerous long conspicuous stamens, and veined leaves. It seems that Mr. Fretwell also has 'Wilsonii'.

I have a plant of 'Peveril'. I reproduce in Plate 223 a photograph of a young flower of 'Peveril' with a more mature flower of *wilsonii* 'Hergest', 'Peveril' is on the left and 'Hergest' the right. It was not possible to match the maturity of the flowers but the two are identical as are the veined leaves (Plate 224); 'Hergest' is on the left and 'Peveril' the right.

We can conclude that 'White Fragrance' has no link with E. H. Wilson's, but *C. wilsonii*, Hergest form and 'Peveril' are the original *C. wilsonii* of E. H. Wilson.

The two *wilsonii* 'White Fragrance' and the true *wilsonii* have caused much confusion. The plant described as *C. wilsonii* by Christopher Grey-Wilson, *Clematis. The Genus* (p.86 and Plate 48) seem to be 'White Fragrance'. In the *Clematis Register and Checklist 2002*, *C. montana wilsonii* is described under 'Peveril'. Under *montana* var. *wilsonii* 'Sprague' there is described a scented clematis – presumably the other *C. wilsonii* ('White Fragrance'). This seems to follow the description given in Magnus Johnson *The Genus Clematis*, p.402. I add a photograph of the alleged (deeply scented) *wilsonii* ('White Fragrance') for comparison (Plate 225). The long tepals folded at the middle, irregular shape of flower in a number of ways, overwhelming scent, large vigorous plant and flowering at end of main season make it easy to identify.

Clematis spooneri (Clematis montana var. sericea)

This was found by E. H. Wilson in western China in July 1903 and again in 1908 and 1910. 'Spooner' stands for a collector working for Veitch and Son. It is now said to be under cultivation and commercially available. However, Dennis Bradshaw, then Curator of the Montana National Collection, reviewing the group in *The Clematis*, 1993, was the first to draw attention to the fact that most plants under this name in circulation are 'Grandiflora'. Wim Snoeijer supports this view. At various times I have purchased at least six clematis said to be *C. spoonerii*; they have all proved to be 'Grandiflora'.

The original description by Wilson and Sprague is as follows (*Plantae Wilsonianae*. Part III. 1918.):

'Frutex scandens, 3–6 metralis ramis teretibus; ramuli hornotini dense breviter villosi, annotini glabrescentes, castaneo-brunnei, vetustiores cinereo-brunnei; gemmae oblongo-ovatae, densissime villosae. Folia decidua, 3–foliolata, foliola ovata v. ovalia, rarius elliptica, acuta v. breviter acuminata, basi rotundata v. lat, rarius angustius cuneata, plerumque supra medium utrinque dente unico late ovato mucronato instituta, rarius utrinque 2–4 dentata, 2.5–8 cm. longa et 2–4.5 cm. lata, utrinque sericea, subtus densius indumento initio flavo-nitente, maturitate chartacea, firma, costa et nervis supra impressis subtus elevatis, folia lateralia breviter petiolutata paullo minora quam folium terminale longius petiolulatum petiolo 0.4–1 cm. longo, plerumque basi cuneatum; petioli villosi, robusti, 3.5–8.5 cm. longi, ea turionum cirrhosi. Flores solitarii v. bini, e gemmis perulatis in axillis ramulorum anni praeteriti simul cum foliis orientes, albi, 6–8.5 cm. diam.; pedicelli teretes, robusti, 8-–8 cm. longi, dense villosi; sepala 4, obovata v. fere orbi orbicularia, 3–4 cm. longa et 2–3.5 cm. lata, apice emarginata v. mucronata, extus dense flavido-villosa, marginem versus glabrescentia; stamina glabra, stylis paullo longiora, filamentis brunneis compressis linearibus 1–1.5 cm. longis, antheris pallidis lineari-oblongis 3–4 mm. Longis. Achaenia numerosa, ovoidea, compressa, 4–5 mm. longa, brunnea, dense pilosa, stipitata, apice in stylum persistentem longe plumosum circiter 3 cm. Longum attenuata.'

Wim Snoeijer has made the following translation:

'Climber, with round stems 3–6m., young shoots short villous, old stems glabrous chestnut-brown, later grey-brown, bud oblong-ovate, densely villous. Leaves deciduous with three leaflets, leaflet ovate or subovate, rarely elliptic, apex acute (pointed) or broadly acuminate (tapering gradually or abruptly into a narrow point), base obtuse (round) or broad, rarely cuneate (wedge-shaped), usually at the middle or above the middle with one broadly ovate (egg-shaped) tiny teeth, rarely with 2–4 teeth, 2.5–8cm. long and 2–4.5cm. wide, above sericious (silky close-pressed hairs), beneath with glossy yellow hairs, when fully grown papary, firm, midvein and veins above sunken and beneath raised, basal leaflets with short petiolule (leaflet stalk) but the terminal with a longer petiolule 0.4–1cm. long, base usually cuneate (wedge-shaped), petiole (leafstalk) villous, robust, 3.5–8.5cm. long, sometimes curling. Flower solitary or with two flowers together, from buds with bud scales on old wood and above the leaves, white, 6–8.5cm. across, pedicel (flowerstalk) round, robust, 8–18cm. long, densely villous, four tepals, obovate (reverse egg-shaped) or almost orbicular (round), 3–4cm. long and 2–3.5cm. wide, apex emarginated (shallowly notched) or mucronate (very short point), on the outside densely yellow villous, margin more or less glabrous; stamens glabrous, style slightly longer, filaments brownish (Wilson probably has seen old flowers because of the brownish filaments) and flattened linear 1–1.5cm. long, anthers pale linear-oblong 0.3–0.4cm. long. Achene numerous, ovate (egg-shaped), flat, 0.4–0.5cm. long, brownish, densely hairy, stipitate (on a very short stalk), style persistent up to 3cm. long and plumose, long attenuate (wider at the base and thinner to the apex).'

To the original description in *Plantae Wilsonianae* the authors added the following:

'The relatively thick leaves densely covered with yellowish silky hairs, the sericeous flowers and particularly the densely pilose achenes readily distinguish this species from *C. montana* Buchanan-Hamilton and all its numerous varieties and forms. It appears to us more closely allied to *C. chrysocoma* Franchet in which, however, the flowers are pink and produced on the shoots of the current season. The flowers of *C. spooneri* are of much substance and very beautiful. The plant grows naturally in rocky places fully exposed to the sun and is very floriferous.'

The plant has been described again from time to time (*J.R.H.S.Vol.XLV.* 1919.):

'*Clematis spooneri*, a recent introduction from China, is a variety of *C. montana*, from which it is distinguished by the larger size of its white flowers. It comes into flower a fortnight later than *C. montana*, and owing to the greater substance of its petals the flowers are more lasting.'

J.R.H.S.Vol.LX. 1935:

'*C. spooneri* is also sometimes regarded as a variety of *C. montana* (*C. montana sericea*). It too has white flowers but with the outside of the sepals downy with yellowish hairs; the flowers are 3 inches in diameter and the stalks hairy, like the stems.'

Bean, W.J. (*Trees and Shrubs*. 1989.) states:

'*C. spooneri* Rehd. & Wills. In describing this plant as *C. spooneri*, Rehder and Wilson recognised its close relationship to *C. chrysocoma*, to which it is now attached as a variety. It resembles the type in its clothing of yellowish down, but appears to be more hardy and is a more genuine climber in our climate.'
Gorer, Richard (*Climbing Plants*. 1968.) states:

'*Clematis spooneri*. This is a vigorous, but fairly slow-growing climber related to *C. montana*. The young shoots and the stems are covered with down like those of *C. chrysocoma*, but this tends to be silvery and is not nearly so thick. The leaves are rather larger than those of *C. montana* and appear to be more hairy. The flowers are larger, up to 3 in. across, and show the same variation in colour, although the white forms are typical. Even when full-grown the plant will not exceed 20 ft. in height and so it is the best substitute for *C. montana* where space is limited. It flowers in May, usually about a week later than *C. montana*.'

Bartrum, Douglas (*Climbing Plants*. 1959.) states:

'*C. spooneri*. It is classed with the Montana type and blooms about the same time as *C. montana*. It is allied with the Chinese *C. chrysocoma* and has often been described as *C. chrysocoma sericea* (silky). The leaves are clothed with a yellowish, silky down. This deciduous climber attains a height of 20 feet and is a strong, vigorous plant.'
Whitehead, Stanley (*Garden Clematis*. 1959.) states:

'*C. spooneri*. An outstanding species introduced from China in 1909. D. Climber, vigorous to 20 feet, with shoots and stalked, tri-foliate leaves of long, ovate, coarsely toothed leaflets, covered when young with a pale yellowish-brown hairy down of pleasing bronzy appearance when young, and four-sepalled white flowers, 3 to 4 inches wide, produced on long stalks, singly or in pairs from the leaf axil in May–June.'

Is it lost? Are there two similar plants going the rounds – one named *C. spooneri* and the other 'Grandiflora'? Raymond Evison (*Clematis*. 1998.) reports that he acquired a plant from Percy Picton called *C. chrysocoma* 'Sericea' (*C. spooneri*). Later he found that the plant was 'Grandiflora'. *C. spooneri* is deleted from his book. Are the same two plants still circulating one as the true 'Grandiflora' (Evison) and the other 'Grandiflora' (Picton) also but called *C. spooneri*? Nurseries are very careful in their identity of plants but confusion can arise also if there are two different clones of 'Grandiflora' in the same nursery, giving the impression of two different plants. To add to the confusion it is noted that Barry Fretwell (*Clematis*. 1989.) states of 'Grandiflora', that he has seen *C. spooneri* sold under this name.'

The plot thickens. Brewster Rogerson in an article on the website of the International Clematis Society in 2000, states that *C. spooneri* in the United States differs from the English version. (The American version is perhaps a 'Grandiflora') A master of description, Rogerson describes a feature of the English version thus – '…it is overspread with light down, both leaf and stem, and can gleam under a bright sun'.

Christopher Grey-Wilson (*Clematis. The Genus.* 2000.) knows the plant in the wild, denies too close an affinity with *C. chrysocoma*, and regards it as distinct from that plant and *C. montana*, thought it may be a hybrid between the two. He describes it thus –'…having hairier buds and leaves than those of *C. montana*. Sometimes the sepals have a slight flush along the centre…' and '…its general growth and flowering habit is that of *C. montana*, while the pubescence is more akin to that of *C. chrysocoma*, as is its habit of producing precocious flowers on the current year's shoots through the summer months… '.

Christopher Lloyd (*Clematis*. 1989) may have the plant though. He describes it –'…the leaves are broad for their length, downy on both surfaces. The flowers are bold, 8cm. across, odourless. In the clone I acquired from Captain Collingwood Ingram there is a slight pinkish flush along the central veins of each sepal'.

I print the description from *Plantae Wilsonianae* above in the hope that it will help someone identify the plant without doubt and add this desirable plant to our collections.

C. montana 'Grandiflora'

First collected by one of Nathaniel Wallich's collectors at Mount Pundua, Sillet Province, India in June 1829, it was then called *C. punduana*. It is No. 4682 in the Wallich Collection, Kew Herbarium, UK. (See Plate 226) It was given to Veitch of Exeter and flowered there in 1844.

A description and figure of the plant under the name of *montana* 'Grandiflora' appeared in *Botanical Magazine* in 1844. No.4061. Their description is given here for comparison with *C. spooneri*:

'A large climber, with the habit of our own well-known Traveller's Joy, having ternate leaves, and leaflets not very dissimilar in form from that species; but with a very different inflorescence, and blossoms, especially in our variety here given, nearly as large as those of *Clematis florida*. The petioles and peduncles spring in axillary clusters or fascicles, and great numbers from one common point. Leaflets ovate, acuminated, more or less incised, generally with a lateral incision on each side, forming three sharp points, sometimes also coarsely serrated, occasionally entire. Flowers solitary on each peduncle. Sepals spreading large, cream-coloured. Stamens and pistils greenish-yellow. There is no mention of scent.'

C. montana var. *wilsonii*, f. *platysepala*

This plant was found by E. H. Wilson in June, July, and October 1908 and was a variety of *C. wilsonii* with broad tepals. It is not in cultivation as far as it is known. Described in *Plantae Wilsonianae*, 1918, as follows:

'A varietate Wilsonii recedit sepalis late obovatis apice rotundatis v. truncatis'.

To the above is added:

'This form is distinguished by its broadly obovate, rounded or truncate sepals; the flowers are very round in shape and produced at the same time as the leaves.'

Lemoine Montanas

C. perfecta and *C. undulata* were, together with 'Lilacina' produced by Lemoine et Fils of Nancy in 1910. Both lost. See Lemoine Cat. 17:27 (1910) and *The Garden*. 1910.74. 119. Said to be hybrids between *C. montana* 'Grandiflora' and *C. montana* 'Rubens'.

C. perfecta

Described in Rev. Hort. 1911. 244. *J.R.H.S.* 37. 1911. 452. describes it thus:
'Flowers one third larger than *montana* 'Grandiflora' perfect form, wide sepals and bluish-white.'

Kew Bull. **1911.** Page 94
'Bluish-white, larger than in the variety 'Grandiflora'.

Hortus Second. Bailey and Bailey, 1949.
'Bluish-white. Large'.

C. undulata

Rev. Hort. 1911. Page 244 and *J.R.H.S.* 37. 452 refer to it as follows:
'Flowers 7–8cm. diameter, sepals wavy and white, tinted blue'.

Kew Bull. 1911. Page 94 refers to it as:
'Flowers 3–3½in. across, white tinged with blue, and sepals much undulated'.

Hortus Second Bailey & Bailey. 1940. Page 187 refers to it as:
'Large bluish-white flowers'.

Note: It would have been convenient to have found that 'undulata' was 'White Fragrance', but in the latter I find no blue in the flower. Also there is no reference in these descriptions to the overwhelming scent one meets in 'White Fragrance'.

PLATE 226.
Clematis punduana. First collected in June 1829. (See note on page 206.)

INDEX

Page numbers in **bold** refer to illustrations

PLANT INDEX

actinidia, 173, 178–9, **179**
'Albertine', 194
'Alexander', 17, 48–9, **48, 49**, 63, 113–14, **114**, 174
Amherstia nobilis, 39, **40**, 61
'Apple Blossom', 12
'Ballerina' (climbing rose), 195
'Barbara Dibley', 59
'Barbara Jackman', 59
'Bi-color', 125, **125**
'Bill Mackenzie', 12
'Broughton Star', 17, 18, 20, 50, **50, 51**, 80, 109, 121, **121**, 174
'Canary Bird' (climbing rose), 195
'Casino' (climbing rose), 194
ceonathus, 173
'Compassion' (climbing rose), 180, **180**, 194, **194**
'Continuity', 112, 122, **122**, 174, 180, **187**
'Durandii', 12
'East Malling' (syn. *C. rubens* 'E.M.F.'), 16, 56–7, **56, 57**, 99, 116, 117, 118, **118**, 174
'Elizabeth', 17, 18, 20, 58–9, **58, 59**, 60, 70, 83, 87, 92, 115–16, **115, 116**, 174, 177, **186**, 194, **194**
'Elten', 16, 126, **126**
'Filipes Kiftsgate' (climbing rose), 194
'Fragrant Spring', 20, 60–1, **60, 61**, 109, 116, 117, **116**, 174, 177
'Freda', 11, 17, 18, 20, 62–3, **62, 63**, 107, 110, 118, **118**, 174, 194
'Frühlingsgold' (climbing rose), 195
'Galway Bay' (climbing rose), 194
'Gloire de Dijon' (climbing rose), 194
'Gothenburg', 64–5, **64, 65**, 116–7, **116**, 174, **186**
'Grandiflora', 18–20, 68–9, **68, 69**, 76, 83, 108–9, 113, **113**, 125, 128, 174, 180, **180, 186**, 197, 203, 206

'Green Eye', 138, **139**
'Guernsey Cream', 195
'Hagley Hybrid', 91
'Hergest', 202–3, **202**
'H.F.Young', 195, **196**
'Hidcote' (syn. *C. x vedrariensis* 'Hidcote'), 70–2, **70, 71**, 109, 123, **123**
'Highdown' (syn. *C. x vedrariensis* 'Highdown'), 72–3, **72, 73**, 96–7, 123, **121**, 129
'Iceberg' (climbing rose), 194
'Jackmanii', 12
'Jacqueline du Pré', 12
'Jacqui', 20, 74–5, **74, 75**, 78, 94, 120–1, **120**, 174
'Joe', 12
laburnum, 173, **190**
'Lasurstern', 195
'Lilacina', 76–7, **76, 77**, 116–17, **116**, 174, 207
'Madame Grégoire Staechelin' (climbing rose), 194
'Madame Julia Correvon', 12
'Maigold' (climbing rose), 194
'Margaret Jones', 74, 78–9, **78, 79**, 94, 120–1, **120**, 174
'Marjorie', 17, 50, 63, 80–1, **80, 81**, 121, **121**, 174
'Markham's Pink', 12
'Mayleen', 18, 20, 116–17, **116, 117**, 126, 174, 177, **177, 196**, 197–8, **197, 198, 199**
'Meg' (climbing rose), 194
'Mrs George Jackman', 128
'Nelly Moser', 12, 195
'Nevada' (climbing rose), 195
'New Dawn', 16, 19, 8, **84, 85**, 100, 118, **118**, 119, 174, 194
'Odorata', 17, 20, 58, 86–7, **86, 87**, 109, 115, **115**, 174, 177
'Olga', 17, 60, 88–9, **88, 89**, 116–17, **116**, 174, 193, **193**
'Pamela Jackman', 59
'Park Direktor Riggers' (climbing rose), 194
'Perfecta', 76

'Perle d'Azur', **199**

'Peveril' [*C. montana* var. *wilsonii*, 19, 110–11, **110**, **111**, 202, **202**

'Picton's Variety', 11, 20, 50, 63, 90–1, **90**, **91**, 102, 118, 120, **120**, 126, 174, 180, 194

'Pink Perfection', 20, 62, 83, 92–3, **92**, **93**, 107, 115, 116, **115**, **116**, 174

'Pink Perpétue' (climbing rose), 194

'Pleniflora', 74, 78, 94, **94**, 120–1, **120**, 174

'Princess Diana', 12

'Rosea' (syn. *C.* x *vedrariensis* 'Rosea'), **15**, 20, 72, 96–7, **96**, **97**, 112, 123, **123**, 180

'Rubens' (syn. *C. montana* var. *rubens*), **15**, 18, 20, 56, **56**, 60, 76, 83, 98–9, **98**, 102, 116–18, **116**, **118**, 128, 174, 177, **186**, **195**

solanum crispum, 173, 195, **195**

'Starlight Improved', 131

'Summer Wine' (climbing rose), 194

'Superba', 128

'Tetrarose', 18, 20, 84, 100–1, **100**, **101**, 118–19, **119**, 130–1, 174–5, **175**, **187**

'Triternata Rubromarginata', 12

'Undulata', 76, 108

'Unity', **193**

'Veitch', 20, 90, 102–3, **102**, **103**, 118–19, **118**, 174, 194

'Vera', 20, 104–5, **104**, **105**, 116–17, **116**, **117**, 174, **186**

'Warwickshire Rose', 17, 62 106–7, **106**, **107**, 109, 118–19, **118**, 174, 198

'Wedding Day' (climbing rose), 180, 194

'Wesselton', 63

'White Cascade', 109

'White Fragrance', 17, 20, 80, 87, 108–9, **108**, **109**, 113, **113**, 174, 177, 201, **202**, 203, **203**, 207

wisteria, 173, **175**

C. acerifolia, 140

C. alpina, 131

C. anemoniflora, 12, 38, 41, 141

C. brevipes, 140

C. chrysocoma, 13, 17, 20, 52–3, **52**, **53**, 55, 96, 122, **122**, 126, **126**, 129, 130, 174, 180, 206

C. chrysocoma var. *sericea* (*syn. C. spooneri*), 68, 96, 205

C. chrysocoma var. *spooneri*, 19, 129

C. chrysocoma (dwarf), 126, **126**

C. glabrifolia, 140

C. gracilifolia, 17, 20, 66–7, **66**, **67**, 112–13, **113**, 174

C. grata, 43

C. lanuginosa, 10, 81

C. macropetala, 131

C. montana 'Grandiflora', 68, **68**, 69, **69**, 207, 209

C. montana var. *grandiflora*, 13, 43

C. montana 'Rubens', 13, 52–3, 75, 78, 90, 92, 96, 102, 103, 111, 130, 209

C. montana 'Wrightii', 130

C. montana var. *wilsonii* 'Sprague', 203

C. montana var. *wilsonii* f. *platysepala*, 141, 207

C. montana var. *wilsonii*, 13, 19, 20, 174, 200–3, **201**, **202**, 203

C. montana, (syn. *C. montana* 'Alba'), 46, **46**

C. montana, 12, 20, 30–5, **30**, **31**, **32**, **33**, **34**, **35**, 37–3, **37**, **38**, 47–8, **47**, 57, 61, 69, 86, 93, 94, 105, 107, 113, **113**, 129–31, 174, 206

C. perfecta, 141, 209

C. punduana, 68, 206, **208**

C. repens, 110, 200

C. spooneri 'Rosea', 96, 111, 129, 141

C. spooneri (*C. montana* var. *sericea*), 141, 203–6

C. tongluensis, 140–1, **141**

C. trichogyna, 141

C. undulata, 141, 207

C. venusta, 141

C. wilsonii, 75, 108–11, **111**, 113–14, **114**, 174, 201, 203

C. x *vedrariensis*, 13, 96, 129

(★*Plants not yet completely evaluated and at present mainly unavailable.*)

★'Apricot Star', 132, **132**

★'Arguta', 130

★'Brewster', 140, **140**

★'Brookfield Clove', 125

★'Christine', 125, **125**

★'Crinkle', 132, **132**

★'Doctor Penelope', 132, **132**

★'Dovedale' (syn. *C.* x *vedrariensis* 'Dovedale'), 126

★'Dusky Star', 133, **133**

★'El Pinko', 133, **133**

★'Frilly Pants', 133, **133**

★'Giant Star', 131, 134, **134**

★'Hakuju', 138, **139**
★'Hakurakuten', 138
★'Jenny Keay', 74, 94, 131, **131**
★'Joyful Star', 134, **134**
★'Magic Star', 134, **134**
★'Pink Rave', 135, **135**
★'Pink Starlight', 135, **135**
★'Primrose Star', 135, **135**
★'Rhamnoides', 130
★'Rosebud', 136, **136**
★'Senju', 138, **139**
★'Shirley Star', 136, **136**
★'Sir Eric Savill', **127**, 128
★'Snow', 128
★'Snowflake', 138, **138**
★'Starlet', 136
★'Starlight', 131, 137, **137**
★'Sunrise', 137, **137**
★'Superba', 128
★'Sweet Mystery', 136, **136**
★'Unity', 129, **129**
★'Wee Willie Winkie', 137
★'White Rosebud', 137, **137**
★'Wrightii', 130
★'Yuishan' (Jade Mountain), 129, **129**
★ Mitchell Hybrids, The, 131

GENERAL INDEX

Abel, Dr Clarke (1780–1826), 39, 41, 51, 93
Alexander, Colonel R.D., 48
Alpina Group, The, 12
Amherst pheasants, 39
Amherst, Countess (1762–1838), 13, 28,
    38–9, 41, 43–4, 46, 61, 86, 93
Amherst, Lord, 39, 41, 93
*An Account of the Fishes found in the River
Ganges and its Branches* (1819), 29, 34
An Account of the Kingdom of Nepal (1819), 28, 34
Arboretum et Fructicetum Britannicum,
    (1838), 42–3, **42**
Aristocrats of the Garden, 200
Arnold Arboretum, Boston, USA, 110, 111, 200
Australia, 130
Award of Garden Merit, 18, 45
Award of Merit (R.H.S.), 128, 129

Banks, Mr Lawrence, 110
Banks, Sir Joseph (1743–1820), 32, 34, 105
bark (pulverised), 156
Bartrum, Douglas, 205
    Climbing Plants (1959), 205
Bean, W.J., 38, 43, 44, 205
    Trees and Shrubs Hardy in the British Isles
    (1914), 38, 43, 44, 205
Blinkworth, Dr Robert, 38, 44, 46
bonemeal, 157
Botanic Garden (1825–1851), 43, 202
Botanical Magazine, 43, 68, 111, 200, 201, 203, 206
Botanical Register, 43
Boyton House, Wiltshire, 36
Brickell, C.D., 68
British Clematis Society, The, 20, 50, 74
    Certificate of Merit, 50, 74
British East India Company, 28
British Flower Garden, The, 43
British Museum, 36, 38
Brown, Robert (1773–1858), 38
Buchanan, Francis [Hamilton, Francis]
(1762–1829), 12–13, 28–35, 37, 43–4,
    46–7, 51, 57, 61, 77, 105, 141
    *An Account of the Fishes found in the
    River Ganges and its Branches* (1819), 29, 34
    An Account of the Kingdom of Nepal (1819), 34
Burma, 12, 28, 31
buying montanas, 144

Calcutta, 39, 41, 76–7
    Botanic Garden, 28, 30–2, 39, 49, 61, 69, 77
Candolle de, 36, 38, 41 141
    Systema (1818), 141
cane (support), 150, **150**, 192, 193
care of montanas (seasonal), 171–2
Certificate of Merit, 50
Chalk Garden, The, 73
Chapman, Sheila, Abridge, Essex, 129
Chelsea Flower Show, 63, 82
China, 10, 12–13, 31, 34, 39, 52–3, 65–8, 75,
    81, 93, 98, 102–3, 110–11, 142, 200–1, 203, 205
Chinese Wilson, 111
Chitlong, 41
Chrysocoma sub-group, 19, 122
clematis wilt (stem rot), 18, 63, 159
Clematis as a Garden Flower, The, 43

clematis wilt (stem rot), 18, 63, 84, 159
Clematis, The, 130, 201, 203
Clematis, The Genus, 140–1, 203, 207
climate, 142–3
Climbing Plants (1959 and 1968), 206
colour, 174
compost (garden), 145, 156–7, 197
compost (mushroom), 156
container-grown clematis, 147
containers, 197, **197**
Crug Farm Plants, North Wales, 129
cuttings (propagation), 164–7, **164, 165, 166**

Deacon, Mrs Freda, 62, 109
Delavay, Père Jean Marie, 13, 52–3, 129
Denny, Vince and Sylvia, 50
disease resistance, 18
diseases, 159–60, **160**
displaying montanas (see Chapter VI), 173–99
distribution map, **12**
dividing a montana, 168, **168**
Don, David, 12, 36, 38, 41, 57, 141
    Prodramus Florae Nepalensis (1825), 12, 38,
    41, 141
Don, George, 41
double white montanas, 120–1

Early Large-Flowered Group, The, 12
Early climbing roses, 173
East India Company, The, 31, 32, 69
East Malling Research Station, Kent, 56
Edinburgh Botanic Garden, 125
Encyclopædia of Plants, (1841), 36
Evergreen Group, The, 12
Evison, Raymond, 66, 205
    Clematis (1998), 205
Experimental Station, Boskoop, The
    Netherlands, 84, 100

Feeding, 156–7, **157**
    suggested schedule , 157–8, **157**
figures (garden), as supports, 187, **187**
Fisk, Jim, 48, 62, 63, 72, 80, 82, 86, 87, 90, 91, 108
Flora Indica, 3
flowering period, 174
flowering times, 17, 173, **173**
flux, 159, **160**

Forrest, George (1873–1932), 52, 66
Fortune, Robert (1822–1880), 34, 81, 95
Fretwell, Barry (Perivale Clematis Nursery),
    110, 126, 201, 203, 206
    Clematis (1989), 110–11, 201, 203

Ganges, River, 29
Garden Chronicle, The, 128, 129
Garden Clematis (1959), 206
garden plan, 143, **143**
Garden, The, 43, 76, 128, 207
Gardener's Magazine, The, 43, 128
General System of Gardening and Botany, A
    (1831), 41
Genus Clematis, The, (2001), 12, 38
Geographical Society, The, 67
Gooch, Ruth, 78
Gorer, Richard,
    Climbing Plants (1968), 206
Gothenburg Botanic Gardens, Sweden, 64
grass clippings, 156
Gravetye Manor, 90–1
Grey-Wilson, Christopher, 66, 141, 203, 206
    Clematis. The Genus, 140–1, 203, 206
Gubbin, Bridget, 130,
    Growing Clematis: A Complete Guide, 130

Hagley Court, 91
Hamilton (Buchanan), Dr Francis, 28, 30–7,
    37, 38, **38**, 43, 46–7
Hamilton, Colonel John, 33
Hamilton, Francis (Buchanan's nephew), 33
hard wood cuttings, 167
hardiness ratings, 17, 169–70
Henry, Dr Augustine (1857–1931), 75, 98,
    110, 111, 200
Herbaceous Group, The, 12
Hidcote Manor, 70–1, 109
Hill House montana supports, 183–4, **183,
    184**, 193, **193**
honeysuckle, 173
Horticultural Society of London, The,
    (now R.H.S.), 38, 43–4
Hortus Veitchii (1906), 68, 103
host plants, 178, **178**
hot climates, 152
hybridising, 169

Illustrated Dictionary of Gardening (1885), 43
Imperial Botanical Garden (St Petersburgh), 67
India, 12, 32, 33, 38, 39, 43, 46, 68, 76–7, 81, 98, 142, 206
Institution for Promoting Natural History of India, 32
International Clematis Register and Checklist 2002, 10, 203
Jackman's of Woking, Surrey, 54, 58, 59, 92, 128
Jackman, Arthur George, 59
Jackman, George (junior), 59
Jackman, George (senior), 59
Jackman, George Rowland, 59, 92
    Planter's Handbook, 92
Jackman, William (founder), 59
Japan, 16, 138, **138**
Johnson, Göran, 86
Johnson, Lawrence (1871–1958), 70–1
Johnson, Magnus, 12, **12**, 38, 64, 86, 128, 141, 203
    Genus Clematis, The, 12, 38, 203
Jones, Sir William ('Persian Jones'), 31, 77

Keay, Alexander, 131
Kew Gardens, London, 52, 69, 111
King's College, London, 36
Knox, Captain, 28, 29, 31
Kuntze, Otto, 98
Kyd, Colonel Robert, 31

labels and labelling, 143, 153
Lambert, Aylmer Bourke (1761–1842), 34, 35–6, 38, 41, 55–7, 61
    Boyton House, Wiltshire, 36
Lancaster, Roy, 52, 66, 68, 126, 140
    Plant Hunting in Nepal, 140
    Travels in China, 68, 126
Late Large-Flowered Group, The, 12
Late Mixed Group, The, 12
layering (propagation), 160–3, **161, 162, 163**
leaf mould, 156
Lemoine et Fils, Nancy, France, 76, 141, 207
Leslie, Alan, 68
lilac, 173
Lindley, John, 43
liner (first year plant), 145, **145**
Linnaeus, Carolus, (1707–1778), 34, 101, 104
    Species Plantarum (1753), 101

Linnean Society, 28, 33, 35, 36, 37, **37**, 49, 57, 69, 105
Lloyd, Christopher, 87, 109, 128, 129, 206
    Clematis (1989), 128, 206
Logan Botanic Garden, Scotland, 125
Loudon, J.C., 36, 38, 41–3, **42**
    Arboretum et Fructiceum Britannicum, (1838), 38, 42, 43, **42**
    Encyclopædia of Plants, (1841), 36
    Gardener's Magazine, The, 43
Ludlow and Sherriff, 140
    Quest of Flowers, 140

Macropetala Group, The, 12
Madeira, 143
Manual of Cultivated Trees and Shrubs, (1927), 38
manure (farmyard), 156–7
Markham, Ernest, 43, 91, 129
    Clematis (1935), 43
Maund, B. (1790–1863), 43
    Botanic Garden 1825–1851, 43
metal supports (arch, arbour, pergola), 184, **185**
Minto, Lord, 32
Mitchell, Robin and Lorna, 131
Moira, Lord, 32
Montana Group, The, 12
montanas as ground cover, 194
montanas with climbing roses, 194, **194**
montanas, cultivation of (Chapter V), 142–72
montanas, where to buy, 147
Montreal (Kent), 39, 41, 42, **42**, 43
Moore and Jackman, 43
    Clematis as a Garden Flower, The, 43
moving plants, 151
mulching, 88–9, 155, **155**, 191
multiple planting. 180, 192, **192**
Mumford, Des, 130
Musée d'Histoire Naturelle, Paris, 53

nails (galvanised or masonry), 188
Natural History Museum, London, 28, 38, 57
Nepal, 13, 28–30, 32, 36, 44, 46, 49, 105, 142
New Zealand, 85, 94, 131, **131–7**
Nicholson, C., 43
    Illustrated Dictionary of Gardening (1885), 43
nomenclature, 19
non-white double montanas, 121
Northern Liners Ltd., 125

Orientalis Group, The, 12

Pacific Northwest Clematis Society, 140
pale pink single montanas, 115–18, **115–18**
peat (moist), 156
Pennell's Nursery, Lincoln, 74
period of growth, 153
pests and diseases, 159–60, **160**
Philippines, The, 31
Picton, Percy, 90, 91
pink single montanas, 116–18, **117, 118**
Plant Hunting in Nepal, 140
Plantae Asiaticae Rariones, 41, 69
Plantae Wilsonianae, 203–4, 206, 207
Planter's Handbook, 92
Plantfinder (RHS), 128
planting, 144ff.,
 digging the hole, 148–9, **149**
 feeding, 156–8, **157**
 into trees, 151
 labelling, 153
 material layers, 149, **149**
 moving plants, 151
 near walls, 151
 order of, 150
 planning, 143–4, **143**
 pruning, 158–9
 situation, 148
 supports, 150–1, **150**
 soil, 148
 watering, 153–5, **154**
 winter protection, 151–2, **152**
plugs (immature plants, not ready for
 planting), 145, **146**
Potanin, G.N. (1835–1920), 66
Priorswood Clematis Nursery, Ware,
 Hertfordshire, 74
Prodramus Florae Nepalensis (1825), 12, 38, 41, 141
propagation, 160–7,
 cuttings, 164–7, **164, 165, 166**
 hard wood cuttings, 167
 layering, 160–3, **161, 162, 163**
 seeds, 167
protection of plants, 180
pruning, 17, 145, 147, 158–9, **158**
prunus, 179, **179**
Purdom, William, 66

Quest of Flowers, 140

raffia, 188
ranunculaceae family, 10–11, **11**
regular inspection, 153
Rehder, Alfred (1863–1949), 38
 Manual of Cultivated Trees and Shrubs, (1927), 38
repotting, 145
Robinson, William (1838–1935), 91, 128
Rockery Group, The, 12
roofs as supports, 187, **187**
roots, 16, **16**
Rowland Jackman's Planter's Handbook, 58
Roxburgh, Dr William (1751–1815), 28,
 30–1, 49, 77
 Flora Indica, 31
Roxburgh, William (son of the above), 32
Royal Horticultural Society, 43, 45
Royal Society, 32–3, 69

Sale of Goods Act 1979, 147
Savill Garden, Windsor, 128
sawdust, 156
scent, 177
seeds (and seedlings), 167–8
Sheila Chapman Nursery, Essex, 125
single dark pink montanas, 118–20, **118,
 119, 120**
situation, 148
size, 174
Slaktet Klematis, 128
Smith, Dr Harry, 66
Smith, James Edward (1759–1828),
 31–6, 41, 49, 57, 105
soil requirements, 18, 148
Species Plantarum (1753), 101
stem rot (clematis wilt), 18, 63, 159
Stern, Sir Frederick Claude (1884–1967),
 72–3, 107
 Chalk Garden, The, 73
stone and brick supports, 185–7, **185, 186, 187**
straw (well-rotted), 156
structure (of the montana flower), 21, **21**
supports for montanas (including natural
 examples), 181–7, **182, 183, 184, 185, 186,
 187**, 189–93, **188, 189, 190, 191, 192, 193,
 194–9**, **194, 195, 196, 197, 198, 199**

Sweden, King of, 35, 105
Sweet, Robert, 41, 43
   British Flower Garden, The, 41, 43
Switzerland, 94
Systema, 141

Taiwan, 12
Texensis Group, The, 12
Thorncroft Clematis Nursery, Norfolk, 78
training montanas, 188, **188**
Travels in China, 68, 126
Treasures of Tenbury, UK, 54–5, 66, 70, 104, 125
Trees and Shrubs Hardy in the British Isles
(1914), 38, 43, 44, 205
Twelve Clematis Groups, The, 12

United States, 140, **140**, 206
Uppsala University, Sweden, 35

Vedrariensis sub-group, 19, 123
Veitch & Sons (Chelsea), 51, 103, 111, 200–1,
   203
Veitch of Exeter, 68, 206
Veitch, John (Founder, Exeter), 103
   Hortus Veitchii (1906), 68, 103
Veitch, Messrs J. (Kingston, Surrey), 102
Vilmorin, M. Maurice, 52

Viticella Group, The, 12
Voneshan, Albert, 54

Wallich, Nathaniel, Dr (1786–1854), 32, 38,
   41, 46, 61, 68–9, 77, 111, 206
   Plantae Asiaticae Rariones, 41, 69
Wallich Collection, Kew Herbarium, UK,
   38, 68, 206
walls as supports, 186, **186**
Ward, Dr Nathaniel, 95
   Wardian Case, the, 34, 81, 95, 97
watering, 153–5, **154**, 197
Wellesley, Lord, 32
Wellington, Duke of, 32
Westleton, Suffolk, 48, 80
white single montanas, 113–14, **113, 114**
Whitehead, Stanley B., 43, 205
   Garden Clematis (1959), 44, 205
Williams, Jacqui, 74
Williams, John, 106
Wilson, E.H. (1876–1930) 13, 51, 68, 71, 75,
   98, 103, 108, 110, 111, 200–1, 203, 207
   Aristocrats of the Garden, 200
   More Aristocrats of the Garden, 109, 111, 200, 203
winter protection, 151–2, **152**
wire (plastic coated), 188
wood supports (poles/posts), 181–4, **181, 182, 183**